CALENDARS

365

THREE HUNDRED AND SIXTY FIVE

Calendar Designs with a Twist

SendPoints

JAN 1 — New Year's Day

FOREWORD

Ever wondered how different the world will be without calendars? Try arranging meetings with your colleagues, remembering the anniversaries and birthdays of your loved ones, or booking your next vacation without the help of a calendar. Thinking back, we are truly grateful to renowned historians, astronomers and kings (yes, kings) for giving us the humble calendar that we so rely on today.

Speaking of kings, Julius Caesar introduced the calendar in 45 BC with it starting on the 1st of January. The word calendar was derived from the Latin word of the first day of every month — *kalendae*. Today, the calendar that we used was named after Pope Gregory XIII in 1582 and is commonly referred to as the Gregorian calendar.

What is a calendar and how it works? A calendar is a system of organizing days for social, religious, commercial or administrative purposes. This is done by giving names to periods of time, typically days, weeks, months, and years. A date is the designation of a single, specific day within such a system. Periods in a calendar (such as years and months) are usually, though not necessarily, synchronized with the cycle of the sun or the moon. Many civilizations and societies have devised a calendar, usually derived from other calendars on which they model their systems, suited to their particular needs.

Today, the modern calendar takes on more roles than just keeping track of the present day, month and year. It has also evolved into a tool to plan daily activities; staying organised so that productivity can be; remembering birthday and keep commitments; know important festival dates; as well as setting schedules and meeting deadlines. With the advent of modern technology, these calendars have evolved from being hung on the wall to finding its place inside gadgets such as laptops, tablets and smartphones. In response to these advancements in technologies, the design of these calendars have also been challenged—to design ergonomic and user friendly Graphic User Interface for interactive calendars; as well as to provide creative solutions to the physical calendar.

Besides being a tool of measuring time and organising dates, calendars can also be a great way to promote your own portfolio or product. Companies and organisations will print calendars annually with their logos and contact information on them, reminding people of their services and products when placed on the desks of the recipients. More recently, design studios have also crafted their own calendars, often based around a theme or their expertise in crafting methods, such as illustrations, graphics, or even letterpresses and silk screens.

From telling time and organising our schedules, to promotion and design, the calendar have come a long way in providing us a more concise concept of time and dates. This book, *Three Hundred and Sixty Five*, curates these calendars into four chapters, divided into four themes based around the seasons. Spring showcases calendars that are associated with rebirth, renewal and the colour yellow; Summer presents to us the happiest calendar designs and the calendars that are mostly of a green and light blue hue; Autumn is the season of harvest and showcases the calendars that contain warm colours such as orange and brown; lastly, Winter showcases calendars that are geometrical, with cooler colours such as blue and white. The book has 366 pages, with every page representing a day in a year. The running headers on the side edge of the book also reveal the holidays and special events being observed on that day.

In this showcase of great calendar designs, *Three Hundred and Sixty Five* will provide a good selection of examples that offers a unique and innovative touch to one of the most traditional of products—the calendar.

JAN 3

First day of school (Singapore)

CONTENTS

SPRING 5
SUMMER 71
AUTUMN 175
WINTER 273
INDEX 359

JAN 4

World Braille Day

JAN 5 — National Bird Day (United States)

SPRING

JAN
6

Armed Forces Day (Iraq)

2015 Calendars

Studio Project 53
Design Charlotte Allen

In spite of all the digital calendars available on desktops and phones, there is something about the hands-on nature of products that people like. Printed calendars reveal the texture, details and subtleties that most of us miss. With the run up to the New Year, Project 53 designed a limited run of calendars, intended to brighten up your walls that are a far cry from the standard linear fashion calendars you are likely to find in many of your local high street stores. You could take your pick with two variations, so if the standard dates and days of the week calendar wasn't enough, there was the alternative calendar for scribbling in your all-important reminders. Fresh from the printers, these A2 sized calendars, available in either a mustard or navy colour, were screen-printed on 300gsm uncoated stock for a tactile finish.

Patties* About Artiodactyl's Life

Studio Adequate People
Design Elina Zolotareva
Photography Elina Zolotareva

"Patty-rhyme" is poetry of pentameter verse size, without rhyming yet funny and a little absurd. Elina Zolotareva portrays noble animals of Russian aphorism and proverbs, such as "horse wearing coat" (meaning uninvited guests), "horses die from work" (meaning useless work) etc. Texts were written in the manner the old Russian poets did: using quill pens, ink, calligraphy.

2012 Summer Planner

Studio   Relay Room

Summer is a bummer if left unplanned, so we decided to right this wrong with our very own planner.

JAN
10

Traditional Day (Benin)

Fedrigoni Woodstock Calendar 2015

Design   Oliver Mills
Photography Oliver Mills

The brief was to design a desk calendar for Fedrigoni to promote their Woodstock paper range to their customers. The calendar needed to be genuinely useful and highly aesthetic, whilst introducing the user to the range of paper throughout the year.

The design is slim to save desk space, and a minimal outer sleeve reveals the vivid colours of the paper range within. Each month is decorated with a unique, organic pattern that is seasonal, and relates to the environmental focus of the Woodstock (that is made from 80% recycled pre-consumer waste).

The quality and versatility of the paper is significant and is demonstrated by the instinctive unfolding and tearing that the calendar requires in daily use. The calendar also features the "Thoughtable", a portable thought used for note taking that fits snug into your wallet, and promotes the Woodstock range.

JAN
12

National Youth Day (India)

2013 WK Goodness Calendar

Studio　　WK Goodness
Design　　Curtis Pachunka (Jan), Nicole Blauw (Feb), Chris Lael Larson (Mar),
　　　　　　Erik Blad (April), Dani Guralnick (May), Peter Yue (Jun), Jason Murray (Jul),
　　　　　　Mike Weihs (Aug), Kristen Minarik (Sep), Paul Levy (Oct),
　　　　　　Sarah Hollowood (Nov), Ben Guernsey (Dec), Brad Simon (Cover)
Letterpress　Chelsea Parker Guidry

Each year, our studio releases a limited edition custom calendar to celebrate our talents. Each month is designed by a different studio artist. For 2013, we decided to make a calendar which would continue to be useful even after the year had passed by printing each month on a reusable paper coaster. Each designer was asked to create a design unique to their respective month using a uniform Pro-colour palette, which was then printed by hand on a Chandler & Price platen press in our Portland, Oregon studio.

JAN 14

National Forest Conservation Day (Thailand)

Wandplaner & Wandkalender

Studio DiG / Plus GmbH
Design Karsten Heller, Hanno Dannenfeldt
Photography Anne Deppe

The idea of a "Simple-As-Can Home Organizing Tool" was created in 2002 by two graphic designers and entrepreneurs of our design studio in Berlin. It comes with a German and an English side, with the English Side is changing its colour every Year. 100 Post-Its© with a hole helps you to mark important dates. The smaller calendar is rolled in tissue Paper, while the double sized planner is folded down to 1/12 of its size, so that the months fits within the folded lines. Both products were printed on recycled paper (carbon-neutral), packed in materials from renewable raw materials and processed from carbon-neutral sources.

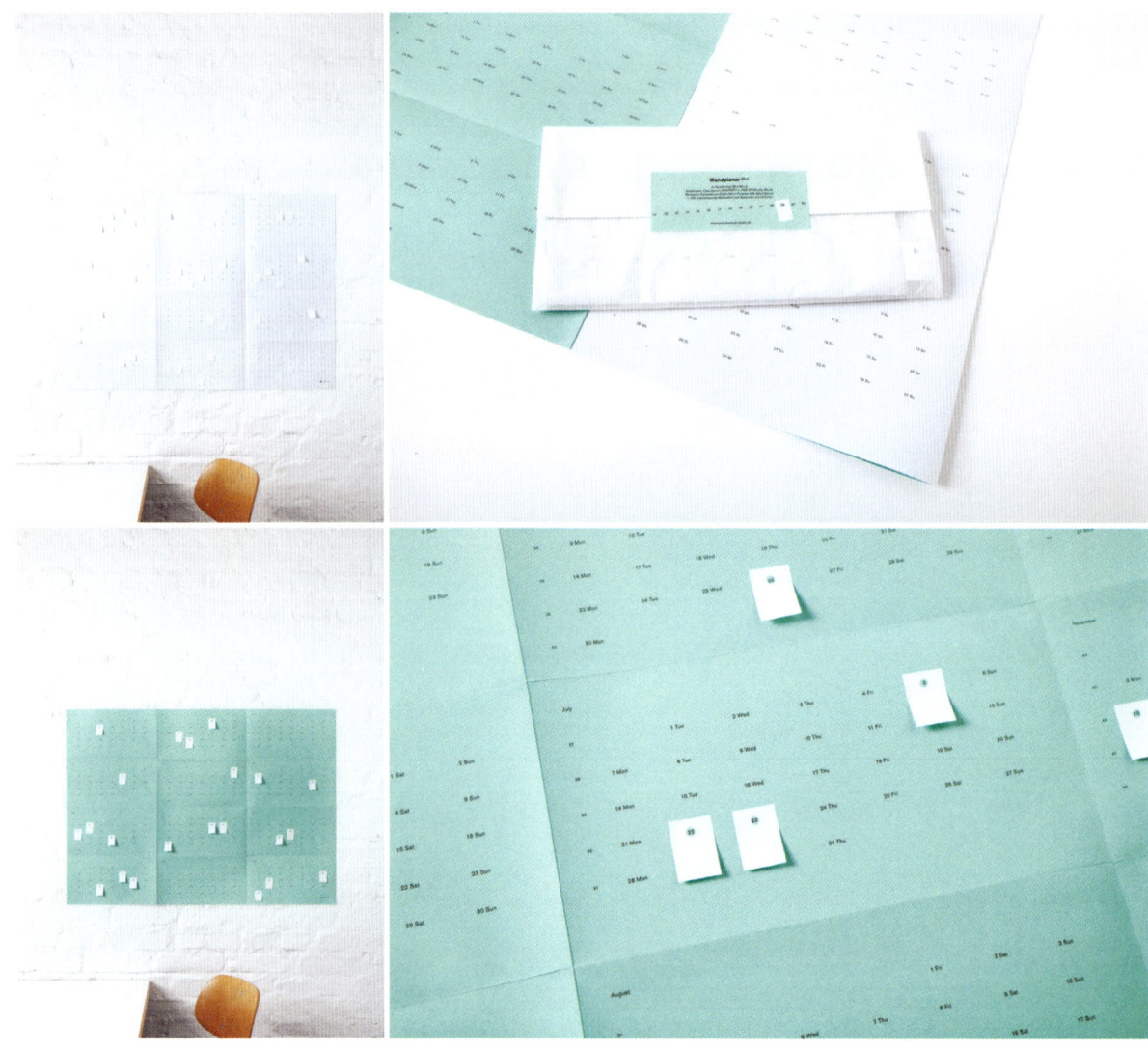

JAN
16

Teachers' Day (Thailand)

2014 DoD Calendar

Studio   The Leo Burnett Dept. of Design
Director of Design   Alisa Wolfson
Design Direction   Alex Fuller, Natalia Kowaleczko
Design   Remy Glock

Our Assignment: Develop an interactive and functional holiday gift for our office partners utilizing minimal resources.

Our Approach: We transformed a standard tabloid sheet into a fold-able calendar that fits snugly under our company monitors. We mixed and matched colours to vary and personalize the gift. The calendar also includes major corporate holidays listed on the packaging, indicated by a small dot on the day.

JAN 17 — National Day (Minorca)

Camouflage

Studio 3EyedBear

Paper-toy calendars for 2013. This little camouflaged puppy-desktop-kit forecasts all the dates and days for the whole year of 2013. As this was created when the Mayan calendar just is about to end, we figured that lots of people are in desperate need for a new one.

JAN 19

Theophany / Epiphany (Eastern and Oriental Orthodoxy)

Calendar Card Deck

Design   Chelsea Phillips
Photography Chelsea Phillips

This calendar was designed to stray away from the standard grid organization and present itself as a multifunctional item. A deck of cards contains 52 cards, four suits, and 13 cards in each suit. A standard calendar year contains 52 weeks, four seasons, and 13 moon phases in each season. Coincidentally, these two systems could co-exist.

The Calendar Card Deck is a tabletop calendar that displays one week at a time in a wooden slot. The rest of the deck is held in the attached box. Each card includes blank spaces next to each day, which allow space for written reminders and important dates. At the end of the week, you would "discard" the current week to the back of the deck. At the end of the year, you have a usable card deck as well as a memory book of the year's events.

JAN
22

Reunion Day (Ukraine)

Mos Burger 2010 Calendar

Design Onion Design Associates
Illustration Cheryl Lin, Wei Kao, David Chou

A self assembled calendar created for MOS Burger. Each month is represented by an item of their menu.

JAN
24

Unification Day (Romania)

Year Planner 2014

Design Crispin Finn
Photography Crispin Finn

This year's planner displays each month in alternating colours and are presented as separate bars for easy reference. The boxes are large enough to allow for annotations for everyday. UK public holidays and GMT daylight time saving dates are marked with icons, and US holidays are listed in the information at the lower edge of the planner. The design is intended to be highly functional but easy on the eye and is screen-printed in our trademark colours — red, white and blue.

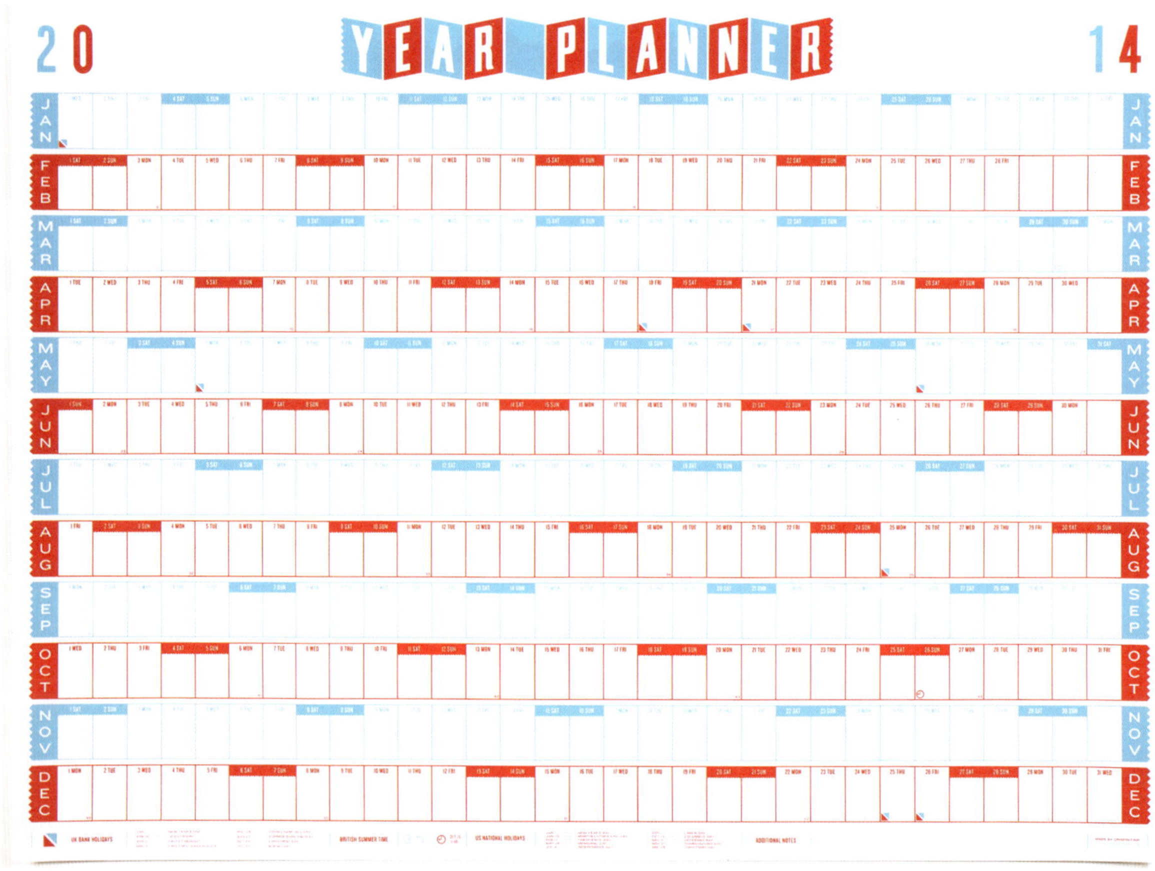

Safari

Studio good morning inc.
Art Direction Katsumi Tamura
Design Takahiro Sugawara
Copy-writing Toshiyuki Nagamatsu

Safari is a paper-craft animal calendar, where you can remove and assemble the six sheets with two monthly calendars on the sides. Fold the body and the joint sections along the creases, look at the marks on the joints and fit together as shown. Quality designs have the power to modify space and transform the minds of its users. They offer comfort of seeing, holding and using. They are imbued with lightness and an element of surprise, enriching space. Our original products are designed using the concept of "Life with Design".

International Customs Day

International Day of Commemoration in Memory of the Victims of the Holocaust

Town

Studio	good morning inc.
Art Direction	Katsumi Tamura
Design	Takahiro Sugawara
Copy-writing	Toshiyuki Nagamatsu

Town is a paper craft kit with parts that can be freely assembled into a calendar. Put together buildings in different forms and enjoy creating your very own little town. Quality designs have the power to modify space and transform the minds of its users. They offer comfort of seeing, holding and using. They are imbued with lightness and an element of surprise, enriching space. Our original products are designed using the concept of Life with Design.

Calendar 2015

Design Studio Servaas

My starting point was to design a calendar as a "spatial pattern", as a calendar year can be perceived as a repeating spatial pattern. The result is a functional and simple fold-able pocket calendar, small in size and easy to bring with you. It can be unfolded in one movement, which enables you to see an overview of the year as well as revealing a colourful, spatial pattern. You can use this calendar on your desk, hang on your wall or take it with you in your pocket.

JAN 28

Data Privacy Day

MINIATURE CALENDAR

Design   Tatsuya Tanaka

Everyone must have had similar thoughts at least once. Broccoli and parsley might sometimes look like a forest, or the tree leaves floating on the surface of the water might sometimes look like little boats. Everyday occurrences seen from a pygmy's perspective can bring us lots of fun thoughts.

I wanted to take this way of thinking and express it through photographs, so I started to put together a "MINIATURE CALENDAR." These photographs primarily depict diorama-style figures surrounded by everyday items. Just like a standard daily calendar, the photos are updated daily on my website and SNS page.

Beer Salt 2014 Calendar

Design　　　Whiskey Design
Printing　　　Vahalla Studios
Photography　Austin Walsh Studio

Twang Beer Salt is the original, premium flavoured salt that combines the tradition of adding citrus and salt to beer for a little flavour punch. For a product that is one of a kind, sometimes you just have to get people to try it before they can love it. And since a lot of Beer Salts' demographic loves music festivals, spring break trips, NASCAR races and tailgating, Twang brings the party to them. This seasonal calendar showcases some of the most exciting field events hosted by Beer Salt, along with some other holidays that calls for a party. The bright, clever illustrations depict all the shenanigans one might encounter while celebrating events year-round with Twang. The poster can be rotated each quarter to better view the different events and illustrations showcased each season.

SNUG.TOYBLOCKS 2015

Design   SNUG.STUDIO

Graphical calendar with numbers laid out to resemble the months built like toy blocks.

FEB 2 — World Wetlands Day

Calendar 2013

Studio Reboot Creative Agency
Design Katerina Mahaira, Evi Mahaira
Photography Reboot Creative Agency

2013 Calendar is a dynamic, vintage-like calendar. 2013 was the happy first year of our office, so this calendar was designed to bring joy in each month with inspirational quotes.

Old vs new is our motto, so we decided to combine the '60s & '70s poster style with a modern one, filling it with various fonts, while also trying to give it a harmonious feeling. By designing this calendar, we hoped for 2013 to be a sweet and joyful year.

Allegheny Financial 2012

Studio   Bunch

2012 Annual Planner for Allegheny Financial. The combination of yellow pages tied together with red thread in a sewn binding with an open spine stitch was matched on the cover by using red and holographic foil, one over another.

FEB 5

National Weatherperson's Day (United States)

This Year 2014

Design This Studio

Each year we create a typographic calendar. We set ourselves simple rules and they are always use the same two weights of typeface. Look at how the information can be laid out and always printed with Black and one PMS on an A1 sheet.

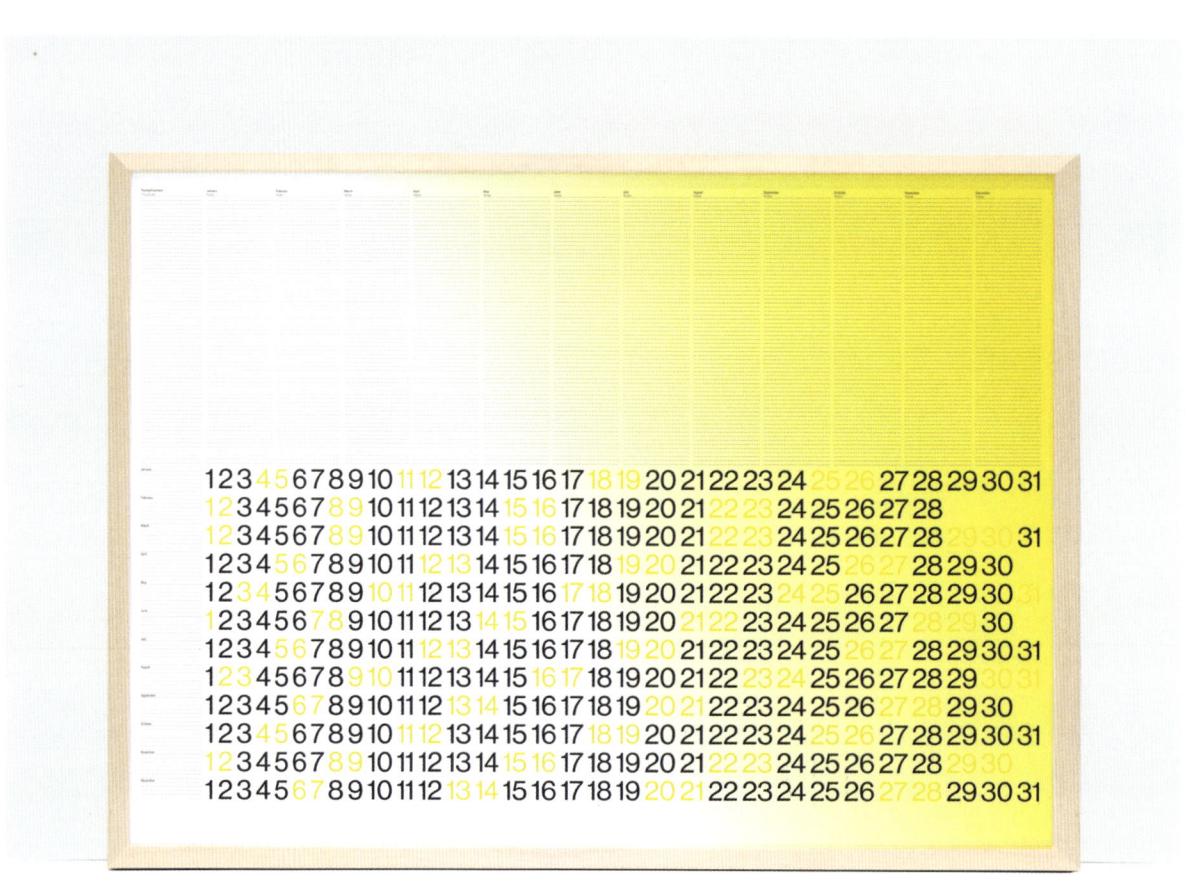

The Concept of Corporate Calendar of Plastic

Studio   eliasdesign.ru
Design   Ilya Ayakov
3D Rendering   Ilya Ayakov

The corporate calendar is made from plastic, by laser cutting and bending plastic. The calendar table includes the dice that shows the date, from 1 to 31 and plastic panels showing the months. In the back there are holes for writing utensils. This concept has great opportunities for a variety of branding.

Independence Day (Grenada)

Life Calendars: How Was Your Day?

Studio Wap-oh!
Design Raquel Catalan

Life Calendar: How was your day? is a funny and unique calendar in which you can reflect graphically your every day mood. It can be used as a mini personal diary of life experiences and help us to be conscious with our own wellbeing.

Each day can be represented by a clear emoticon face to draw how you felt that day. Five moods are suggested: very good, good, normal, bad, very bad. You can also draw many other faces or even include little notes that you might want to remember.

The calendar is valid for any year. There are 365 emoticon faces in the calendar, one per day, numbered and ordered by month. You can start the first day of the year or in any special date, like for example an anniversary. Once finished, the calendar becomes a very personal keepsake that can decorate a special corner of your home.

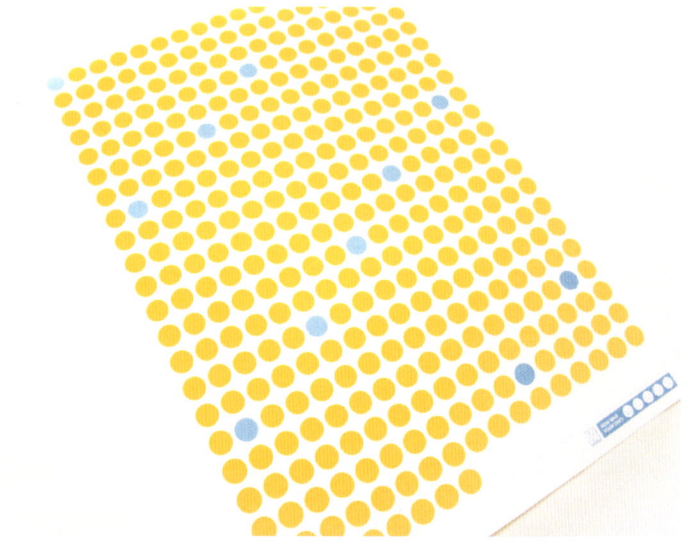

FEB
9

Stampd

Studio   Brandberry
Creative Direction   Valera Namazov
Lettering Artist   Natasha Nikulina
Photography   Natasha Nikulina

We always been interested in having our own studio calendar for internal use. We could just print nice pictures on paper, add numerals, stitch it and here it is, a calendar for 2013 is ready. But it is not interesting to work on and we would like to come up with something special.

Thus, the idea occurred to a create universal STAMPD calendar. Each month, we developed custom lettering and individual stamps was made. Any paper surface can be turned into a calendar just in two actions. Magazine pages, napkins, stickers, printed illustrations — everything can become a calendar. We are not limited by the number of copies and there is the possibility to make as many various calendars as your imagination allows.

FEB 11

World Day of the Sick

42

FEB
12

Darwin Day

FEB
13

Hug Day

Doggies Wall Calendar for 2014

Studio　　　Polkka Jam
Design　　　Kristina Haapalainen, Sami Vähä-Aho
Illustration　Kristina Haapalainen, Sami Vähä-Aho
Photography Tuula Aikioniemi, Lauri Hannus

Doggies Wall Calendar features 12 illustrated pages inspired by a man's best friend. Every month, we illustrated the lovely character of the particular dog/dogs in a situation that is or could be typical for them. The rugged Scottish deer-hound Himmur as October's dog and dandy poodle Ossi of November among others.

We illustrated and produced the calendar for our own Polkka Jam collection. Illustrations were made by hand, and colouring and adjustment was made in Illustrator. Calendars are printed on 100% recycled 300g/m² paper. The size of the calendar is 20 × 31cm.

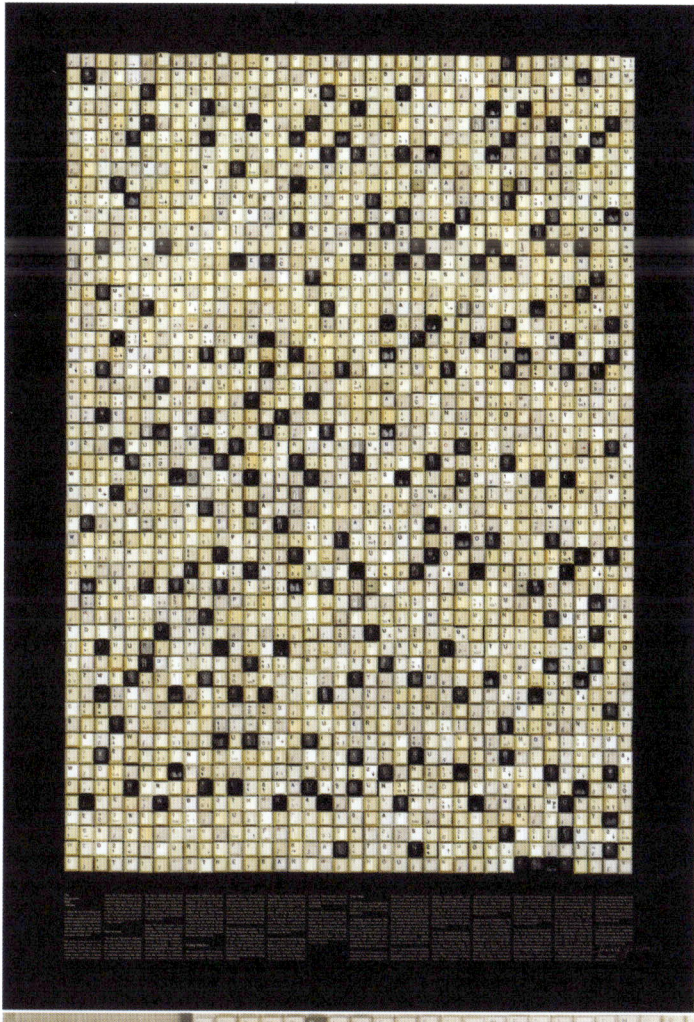

2014 Typographic Wall Calendar

Design   Harald Geisler

The Typographic Wall Calendar is a project I have been working on since 2009. The calendar is made of exactly the number of used keyboard keys (2000 and 14) that represent the year. All keys are arranged manually in a grid (38 × 53 = 2014 keys) to write out all days of the year 2014. The print of the calendar reproduces the keys in original size (1:1).

The initial idea for the Typographic Wall Calendar came from a daydream. In this dream, I imagined a person in a random office typing in front of a computer. The person writes letters, for example to customers. On every letter, the person writes the date — a repetitive part of the job. I imagined that as the person types, the pressed keys would (somehow) sum up or accumulate. Not only would the keys be counted but also collected, ordered and stored. Over days and weeks it would become a mountain of keys. This "mountain of keys" then became the Typographic Wall Calendar.

FEB 15 — International Childhood Cancer Day

A Visual Year — 2014 Calendar

Design The Visual Agency

The calendar includes a selection of events and anniversaries which will occur in 2014. The external ring can be used by the reader to customize his year. The centre of the visualization shows the information related to the weather conditions during the years 2010–2012. Data is specific to the city of Milan.

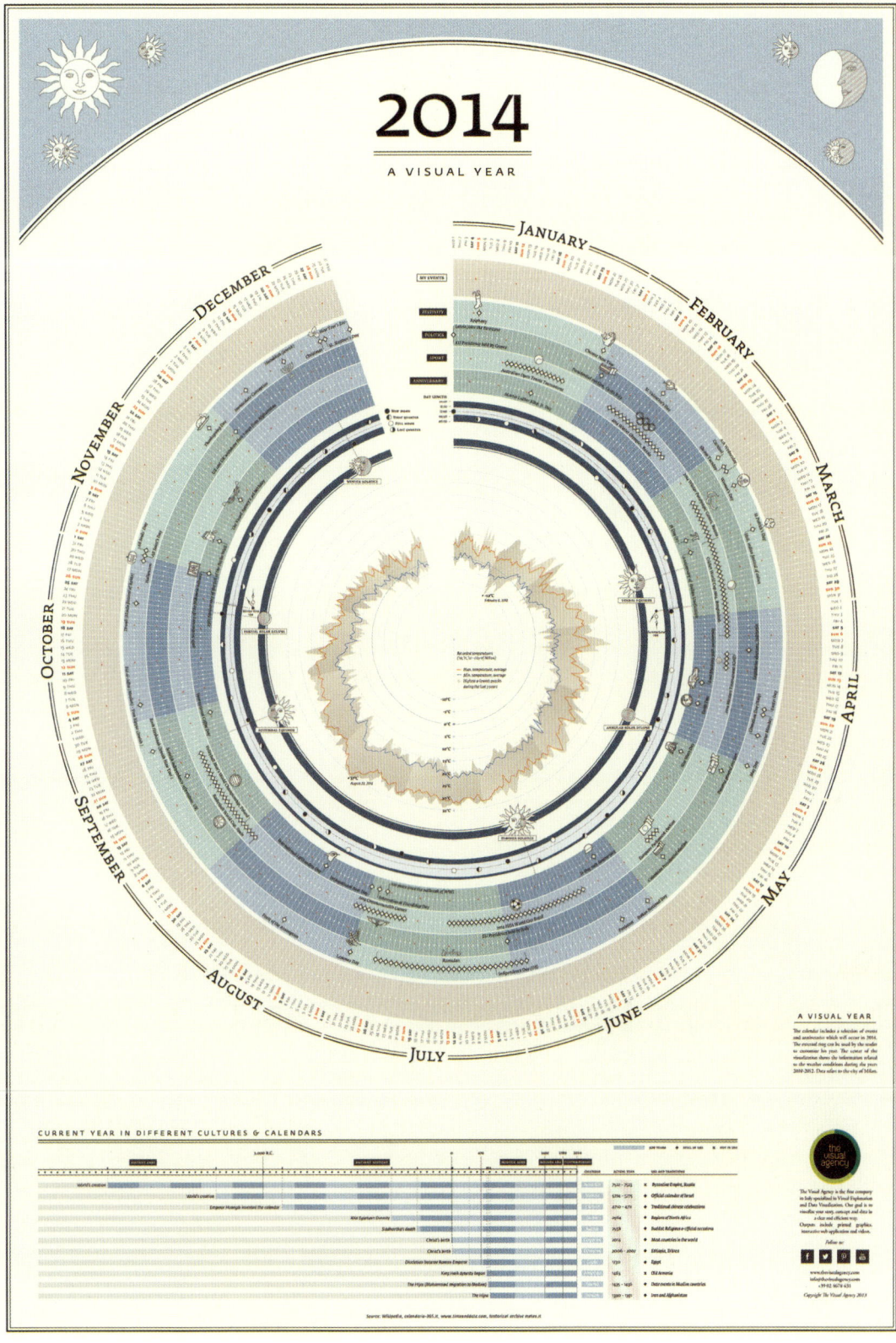

Calendar Tea Towels

Design   Avril Loreti / Modern Home
Photography Avril Loreti / Modern Home

Ring in each new year with my annual hand lettered Tea Towel Calendars!

Making these tea towel calendars is one of my favourite every year. It is a chance to think about what colours I think best represent the upcoming year and what imagery best expresses all the exciting adventures that the new year will bring! Hand drawn lettering is always the signature style for my tea towel calendars. I love sitting down and scrawling out the year over and over again. By the end of the drawing session, I have piles of sheets of paper with hundreds of words to choose from. It is a really great meditative process that makes me reflect on each month and what it has brought in the past and what will come in the future.

This tea towel is great for adding a little art to your kitchen. Fling it over your cupboard door, pull it over your tea towel hook, or frame it and hang it on the wall as art!

Elanders Calendar 2014

Design   Wonder Stuff Studio
Photography Mark Slater

Elanders is a global printing group offering print solutions and cross media marketing to business and industry. We were approached by their UK Head Office to produce a promotional calendar for the brand that would stand out. With Elanders producing the calendar themselves, we were free to let our creativity flow producing a beautiful (and really useful) week-to-view desktop calendar.

FEB 19

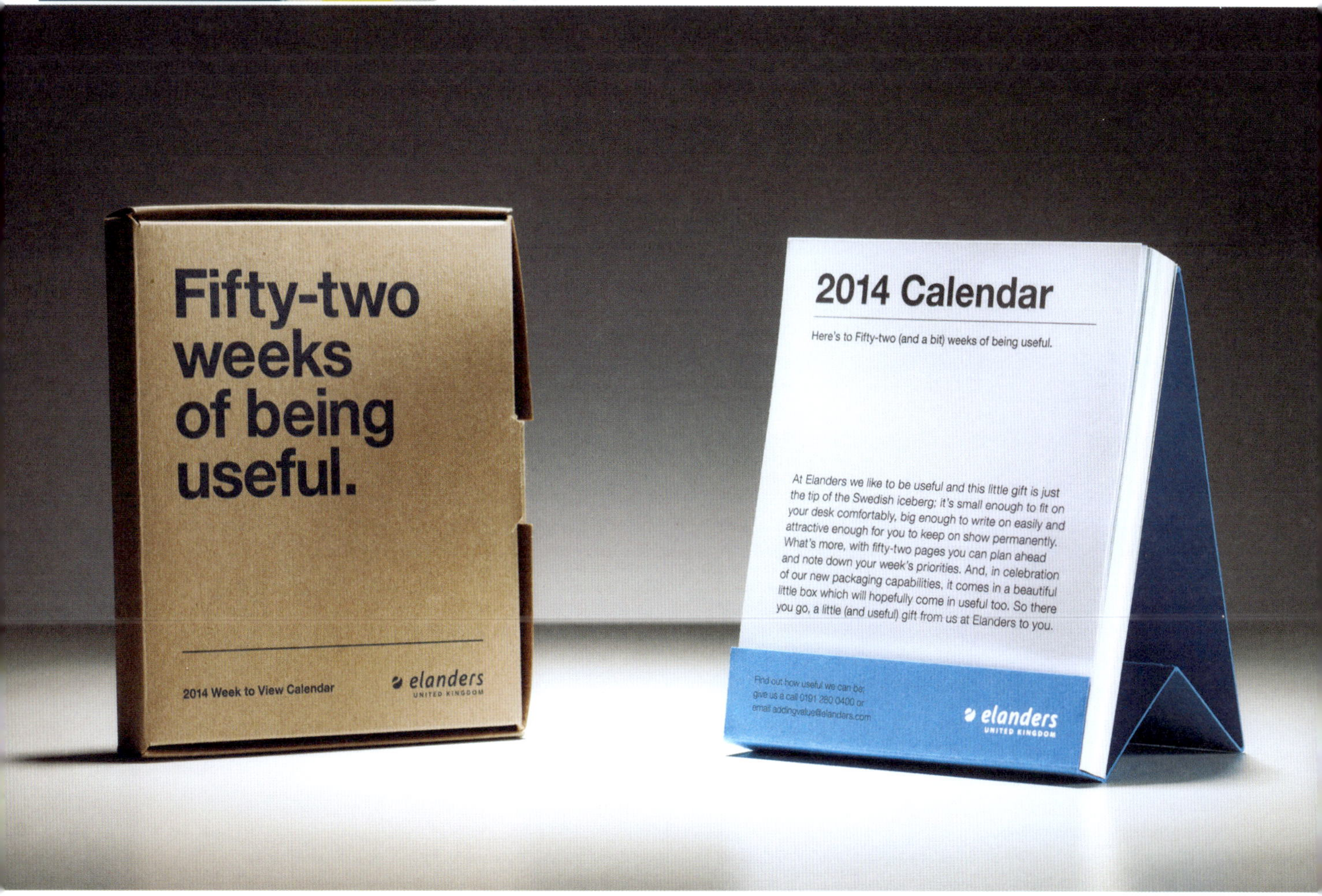

Armed Forces Day (Mexico)

Calendar Kids 2014

Design   Cátia Sá

This project was developed during the graduation of the Graphic Designers in IPCA (Instituto Politécnico do Cavado e do Ave). This calendar consists of 12 months of the year, grouped in four seasons. It aims to familiarize children with the different characteristics of each season, with colours, temperatures and characteristics related to each month.

The seasons were grouped together for three months. Although it does not match the month that starts, the calendar focuses on the months that have more influence. Each season is marked with a corresponding element.

This calendar can work in two ways, one as a poster where you see the full illustration, and another as a triangular-shaped stand which can be used on a desktop. The illustration works well individually as well as in a series.

Botanical Life

Studio good morning inc.
Art Direction Katsumi Tamura
Design Takahiro Sugawara
Copy-writing Toshiyuki Nagamatsu

Botanical Life is a calendar highlighting beautiful plant life in a single sheet. Open the sheet and set it up on the base to enjoy a variety of plant pop-ups. Quality designs have the power to modify space and transform the minds of its users. They offer comfort of seeing, holding and using. They are imbued with lightness and an element of surprise, enriching space. Our original products are designed using the concept of Life with Design.

FEB 23

National Day (Brunei)

Calendar Designs for the Year of 2014

Design Mausam Aggarwal
Photography Mausam Aggarwal

The calendar was designed for Happy Hands Foundation, a non-profit organisation working for the revival of Indian arts, crafts and culture. The main theme of the calendar is 12 Indian tress for 12 months. Every month is illustrated in a way to show the flowering tree of the month, the weather conditions and an everyday little love for the trees.

Month: April
Tree Name: Neem Tree

Month: August
Tree Name: Ber Tree

Month: December
Tree Name: Christmas Tree

Month: February
Tree Name: Semal tree

Month: January
Tree Name: Teak Tree

Month: July
Tree Name: Peepal Tree

Month: June
Tree Name: Temple Tree

Month: March
Tree Name: Gulmohar Tree

Month: May
Tree Name: Mango Tree

Month: November
Tree Name: Ashoka Tree

Month: October
Tree Name: Tamarind Tree

Month: September
Tree Name: Maple Tree

FEB 25 — Memorial Day for the Victims of the Communist Dictatorships (Hungary)

FEB 26 — Liberation Day (Kuwait)

Flowers

Studio   good morning inc.
Art Direction   Katsumi Tamura
Design   Takahiro Sugawara
Copy-writing   Toshiyuki Nagamatsu

Design a room, bring in the seasons — the Flowers calendar comes with a vase design featuring 12 different flowers. Brighten your life each month with a seasonal flower. Quality designs have the power to modify space and transform the minds of its users. They offer comfort of seeing, holding and using. They are imbued with lightness and an element of surprise, enriching space. Our original products are designed using the concept of Life with Design.

2014 Growth & Decay Calendar

Studio   Mink Letterpress
Design   Nicole Lissenden
Photography Nicole Lissenden

A pink magnolia branch blooms and wither throughout 2014 with 12 letterpress prints ranging from one to seven colours.

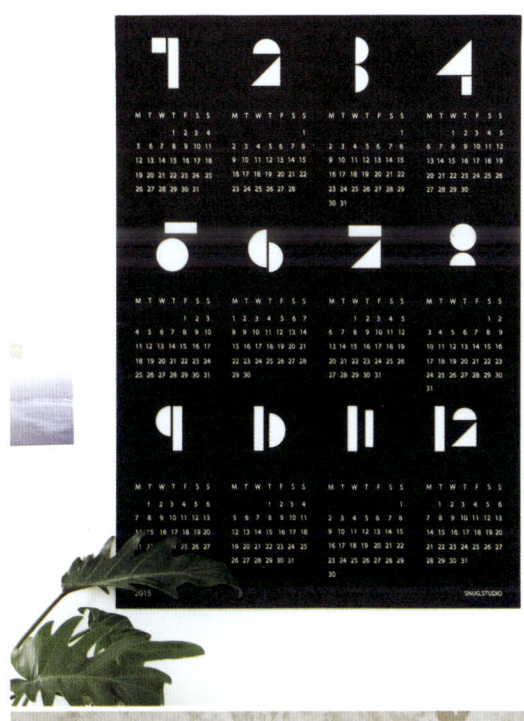

SNUG.VERTICAL 2015

Design   SNUG.STUDIO

June – July – Justify! Wall calendar in oblong size and in full justification.

25th Frame

Design   Liliia Priadko

The calendar was designed for the international festival of animation, "25th Frame". Therefore, it was intended to be funny, interesting and dynamic.

During the creation of the calendar, it was necessary to focus on the theme of animation and movement, which is implied in the name and the logo of the project. It is built on the gamification principle, something like "Rubik's cube". When turned to the right and left, the image changes, creating a new whole picture. Each of the four seasons is a separate illustration of the main character and they differ by colours and seasonal accessories which in their turn interact with illustrating the progress of days, using an unusual calendar grid.

Using this calendar, you can come up with different histories about this character, making it interesting for children and in the office as well.

Farm

Studio good morning inc.
Art Direction Katsumi Tamura
Design Takahiro Sugawara
Copy-writing Toshiyuki Nagamatsu

The Farm paper craft kit is easy to assemble. No glue or scissors are needed. Assembled by fitting together parts with the same mark, each animal will be a two-month calendar. Quality designs have the power to modify space and transform the minds of its users. They offer comfort of seeing, holding and using. They are imbued with lightness and an element of surprise, enriching space. Our original products are designed using the concept of Life with Design.

Kissanpäivät Wall Calendar for 2013

Studio Polkka Jam
Design Kristina Haapalainen, Sami Vähä-Aho
Illustration Kristina Haapalainen, Sami Vähä-Aho

Kissanpäivät (Cat Days or Lazy Days) wall calendar is dedicated for cats and staying in, taking it easy and enjoying the company of our loved ones. Kissanpäivät is Finnish and literally means cat days but it could be translated as lazy days and comfortable and happy life. The calendar have 12 illustrated pages full of cats and lazy day activities.

We illustrated and produced the calendar for our own Polkka Jam collection. Illustrations were made by hand, and colouring and adjustment were made in Illustrator. Calendar is printed on 100% recycled 300g/m² paper. The size of the calendar is 16 × 25 cm.

Mánatal / Moon Calendar

Design   Snorri Eldjárn Snorrason

Mánatal / Moon calendar is a calendar packed with information about each month. The calendar is screen printed on three plates which you turn once every month. The information about the current month will appear through the windows of the upper plate. By concealing all other information it manages to maintain certain level of minimalism and beauty.

The information you can get through the calendar: the current year, the old Icelandic months, the new months, current day of the week, the time, the ratio between night and day, the placement of the moon, constellations and festive days of the month.

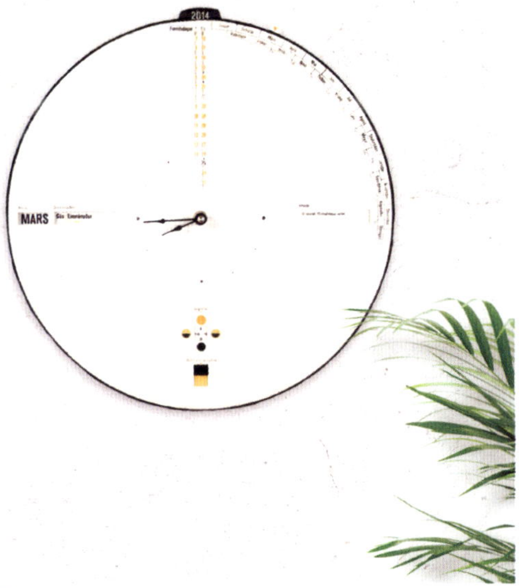

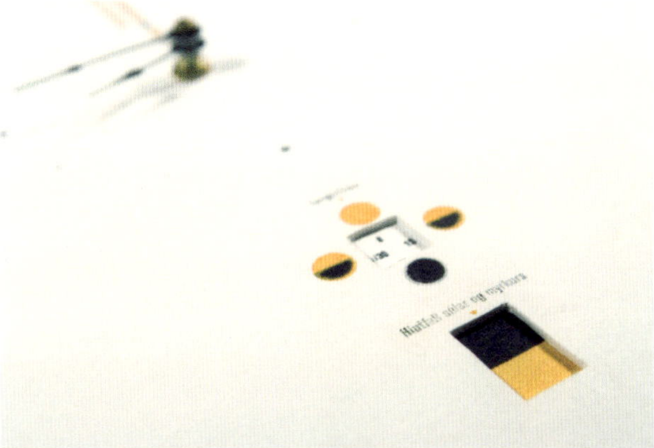

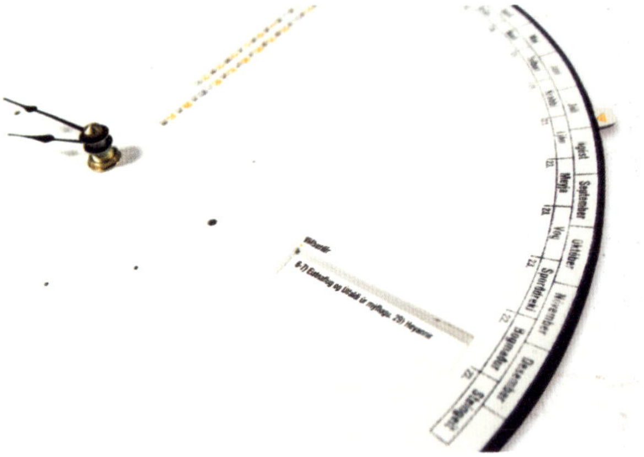

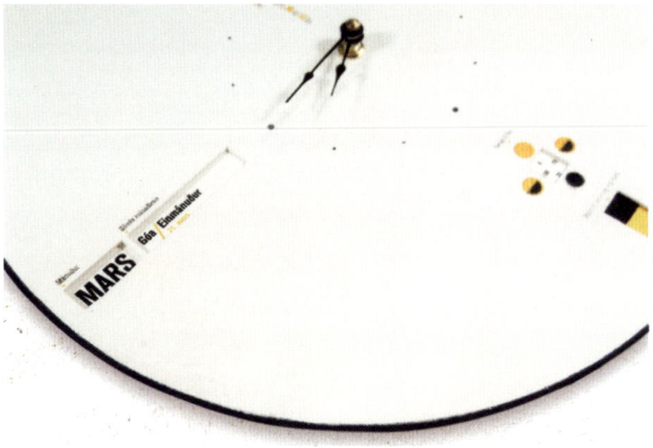

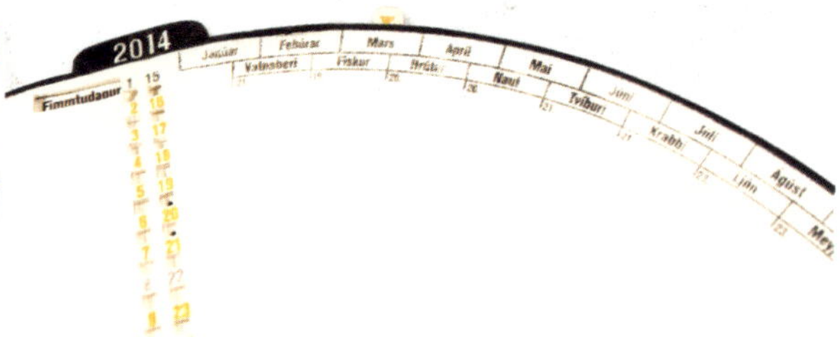

1:X –
Twelve Looks Through the Magnifying Glass

Client Stiftung Palmengarten und Botanischer Garten, Frankfurt am Main (Foundation for the Botanical Garden, Frankfurt am Main)
Studio Hilger & Boie Design
Creative Direction Clemens Hilger
Design Alexandra Gerdemann, Tina Ackermann

Many people do not pay close attention to nature, they see the big picture, the meadow, the forest, the garden. What they do not see, is the biodiversity and the fascinating details. This calendar pays attention and explores the plant with its small characteristics.

The process starts with a visual Petri dish, in which each unique specimen is presented in its original size. Subsequently, enlargements reveal the different structures and shapes. The enhanced plant parts showcased on the calendar sheets have been picked on-site in the greenhouses of the botanical garden. After picking, the plants have been taken apart and digitized with a microscope. The result is a calendar which uses elements of historic biological charts and combining them with a very modern graphic style.

The calendar has been developed in cooperation with the Foundation for the Botanical Garden. It starts in March, on the occasion of a spring gala to raise money for new projects in the garden.

MAR 6 — European Day of the Righteous

1000 Year Calendar

Design Raven Kim

These days people don't seem to think about the little things as long its convenient for them. Many people have to see the calendar to find out which month have days till the 30th or 31st. It made me wonder if convenience is making a fool out of humans, like how people don't know their families or closest friend's phone number without checking on the phone anymore. The concept was to create a sustainable piece made from water bottles, which typically takes thousands of years to decompose. And also to interact with the calendar more often to helps organisation and memories. Different colours of caps represents holidays and special days.

Type Calendar

Design Ryan Ho

The design and creation of a calendar had always been on my design wish-list. I have been wanting to experiment with 3D Typography for awhile, so the start of 2013 was a great opportunity to do both!

The creation of these dates in 3D type was a huge learning process for me. The number of different ideas I had to churn out forced me to experiment with new techniques, like for instance the golden-plated finish of "October"! Admittedly, I am not proud of several of the type-sculptures I've done for a few months, but am eager to do better in projects to come with some of my new-found tricks.

MAR 8 — International Women's Day

Predictions
Calendar Series

Design Tim Wan

Predictions is a calendar series that interprets the definition of "fakery" by tampering with true events; placing them outside their original context to mislead, trigger nostalgia, and remind people of past events.

The design outcomes consists of six 420mm × 594mm full colour double-sided prints accompanied by a 72 page black & white publication that explains the concept and provides further details about the series.

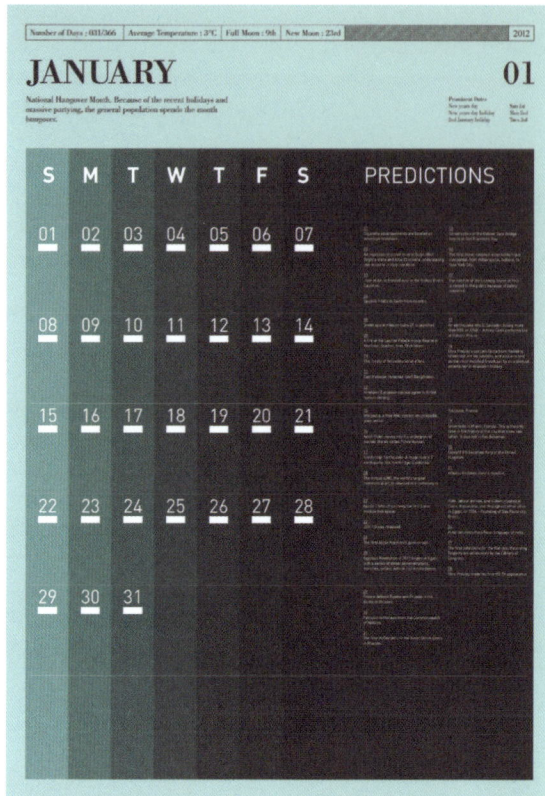

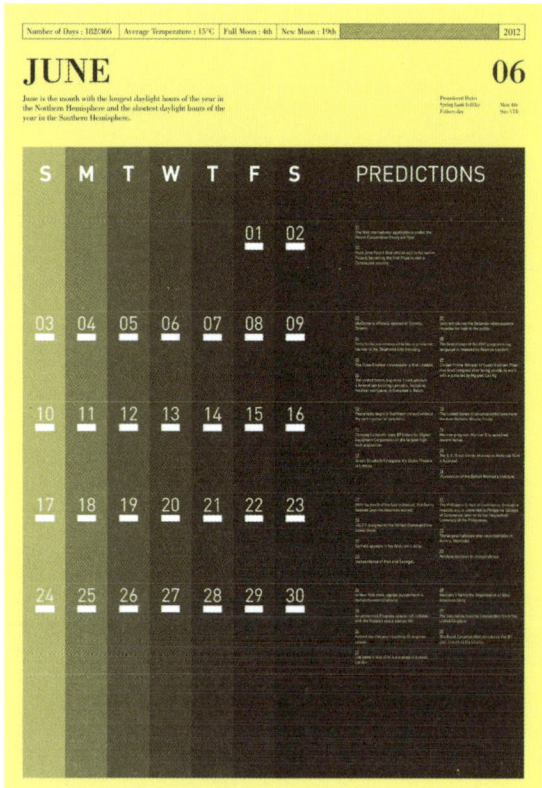

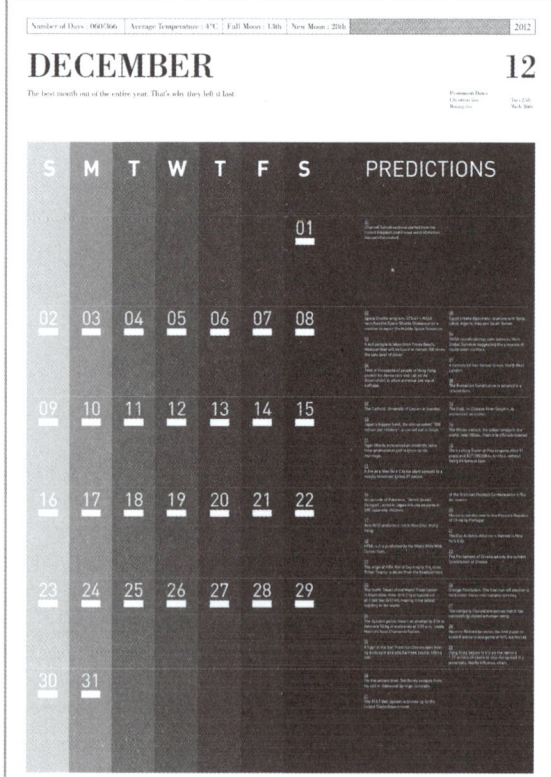

MAR 10

Tibetan Uprising Day

MAR 11

World Day of Muslim Culture, Peace, Dialogue and Film

MAR
12

World Day Against Cyber Censorship

ENJOY YOUR TRIP

Design   Pixelbox Estudio Gráfico S.L.U.

"A cabin in the woods, a desert island, a balloon trip, by train, by submarine… a Delorean, a castaway, an old lighthouse, a mermaid, a volcano, a murderer… Are you ready? The longest trip of the year begins?"

The quote was the idea that time and space are two concepts inseparably related what made me see the calendar as a journey, as a journey through a year of 365 days, as a map in which past, present and future are mixed.

MAR
14

Pi Day

Bingo Card Calendar

Design Retno Hadiningdiah

This project was done as a university project for HPR as a way to raise public awareness on healthy lifestyle. Done in the format of bingo cards, this calendar is meant to encourage people to take part and live healthily in a rather simple and fun way, rather than laying out facts and data that people have already read many times before. Every time they complete an action, they get to cover each box with the specially designed "x" sticker, and eventually win when the desired bingo pattern available at the back of each card is obtained. Different colour schemes is used to mark different season. The size is small enough to be conveniently carried around.

My Zoo 2014

Design Mauresa Hankinson

A fun interactive calendar for all ages. Each month is designed to create a different animal. You just have to follow the diagrams and instructions that are provided to create a fun colourful animal to display the current month.

Eco Gif Package

Creative Direction   Vuk Tatar, Kitchen&GoodWolf
Design   Filip Nemet
Photography   Marko Ercegovic

The Eco Gif Package is both a calendar and packaging at the same time. The calendar can be used over and over again every new year, and contains a bag made of recycled materials and a notebook with some illustrated information about the types of wastes that we deal with in our everyday life. It was a gift for school kids who took part in a project organized by the client, City Administration for Environmental Protection, City of Novi Sad.

Anniversary of the Oil Expropriation (Mexico)

Ideas for the Year

Studio   Phage Limited
Client   Fedrigoni UK

For Fedrigoni's annual desktop calendar, Phage were keen to develop something that gave the traditional printed calendar a new lease of life and relevance in the age of digital calendars and smart-phones.

The result inspires Fedrigoni clients with "Ideas for the Year" in the form of Quick Response (QR) codes, scanned using a free smart-phone app and linking through to an exclusive online portal. Like an advent calendar for the whole year, each week has its own card, with ideas ranging from architectural walks and sculpture parks to exclusive downloads and design events.

Using a different embossed paper each month, and a different colour to differentiate each season, the printed calendar promotes Fedrigoni's luxury papers effectively to a design-aware audience, providing a means of engaging with them, maintaining interest, and staying in front of their mind throughout the entire year.

The calendar won Best Desktop at the 2012 UK National Calendar Awards.

International Day for the Elimination of Racial Discrimination

MAR 22

World Water Day

ETNO (Ethno)

Design TOFU Studio / Poland
Project Iwona Duczmal, Adam Chylinski
Coordination Daniel Naborowski

A non-profit calendar made as a gift for the Gdansk Hospice Foundation. A wide variety of print technologies was used for the calendar: screen printing, hot print, offset print, dedicated die cutting and lacquer print. The calendar won the Audience Award at the International Calendar Contest, VIDICAL 2013.

MAR 24

World Tuberculosis Day

MAR 25

International Day of Remembrance of the Victims of Slavery and the Transatlantic Slave Trade

MAR
26

Purple Day

Interactive Calendar 2013

Design Fooolish Designers

An interactive calendar for 2013. All you have to do is to remove the little stickers every day and reveal the colours throughout the year. At the end of the year, you will be left with a nice poster on your wall.

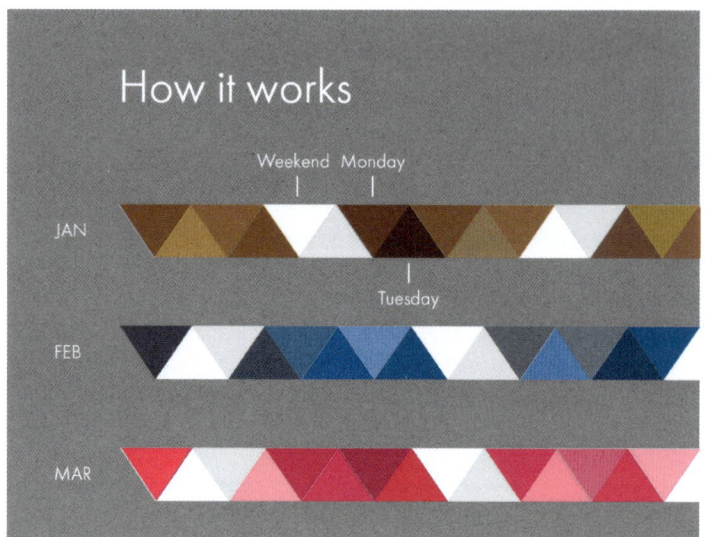

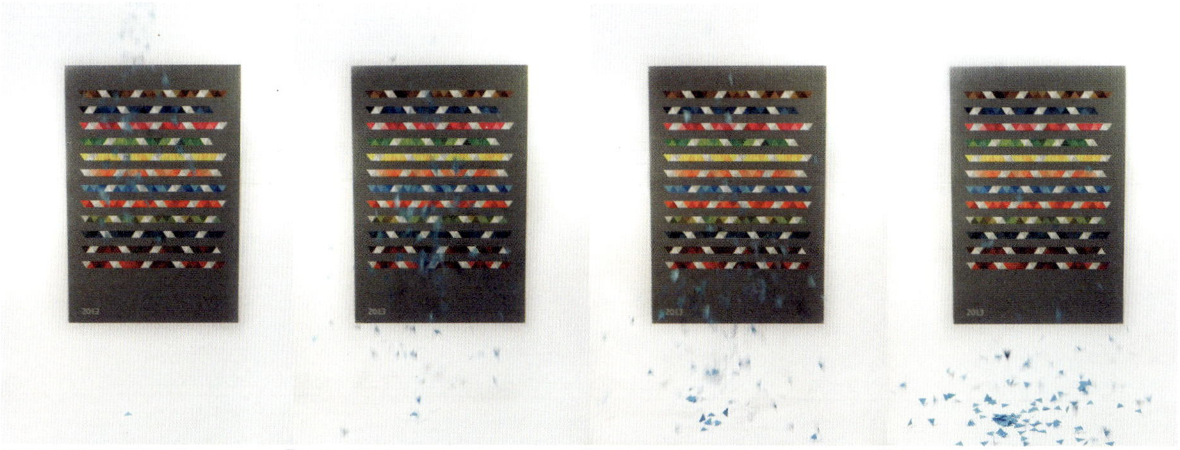

Serfs Emancipation Day (Tibet)

Pull Up Yourself to Face New Challenges

Design   Jennita Shah
Photography   Jennita Shah

An interactive calendar design for the month of January, displaying the resolutions for the New Year in the form of pull-in and pull-out tabs.

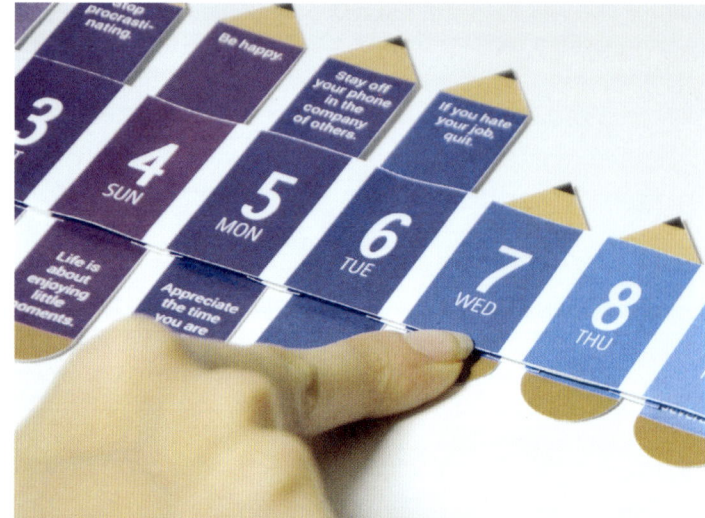

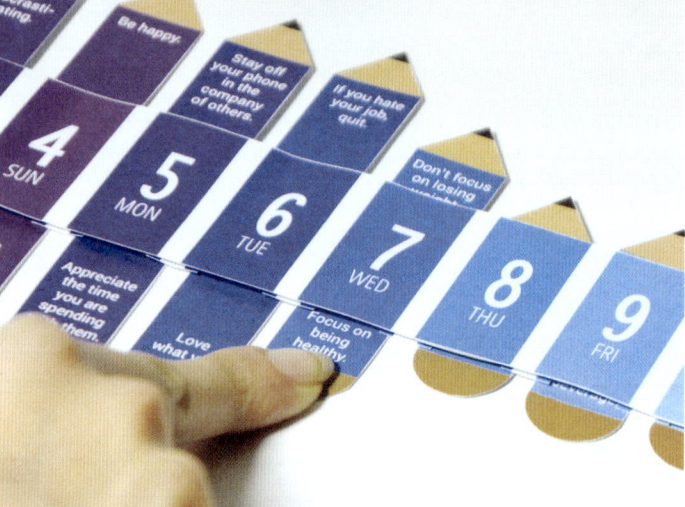

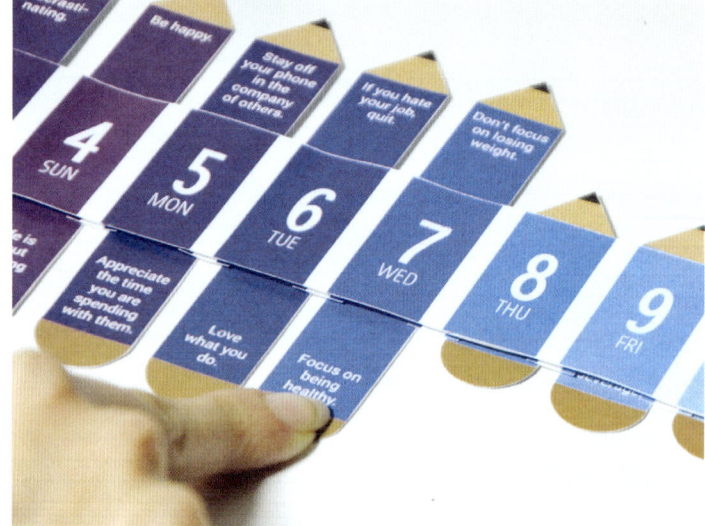

Poster — Calendars 2014

Studio Noblanco
Design Carlos J Roldán
Photography Diana Montoya

A set of four poster-calendars, where every square of colour is a day of the year. The total number of squares is 651, which is equal to 651 days, starting from August 5th 2013 until July 17th 2015. Remembering the '80s childhood with full 8-bit enjoyment.

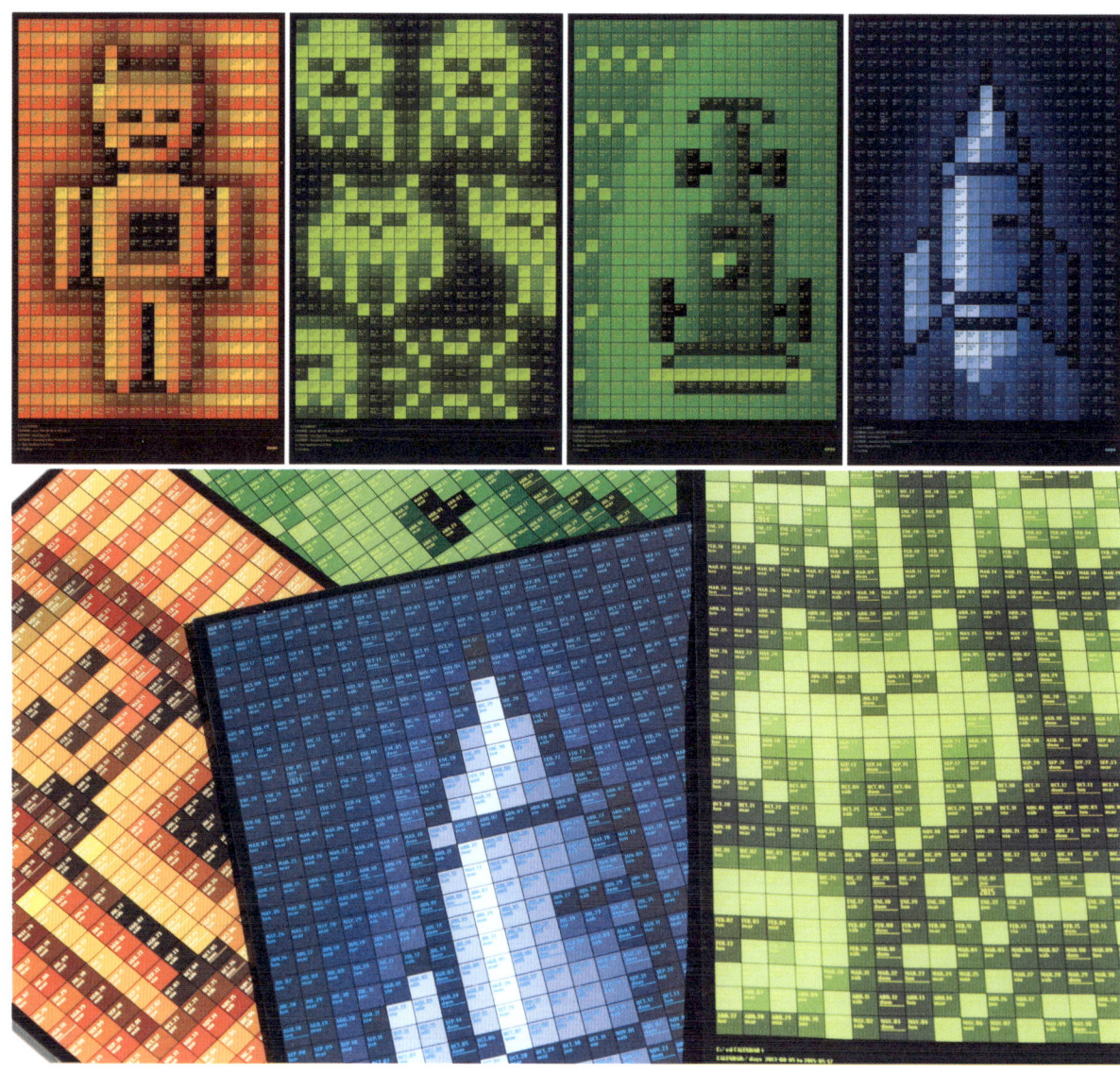

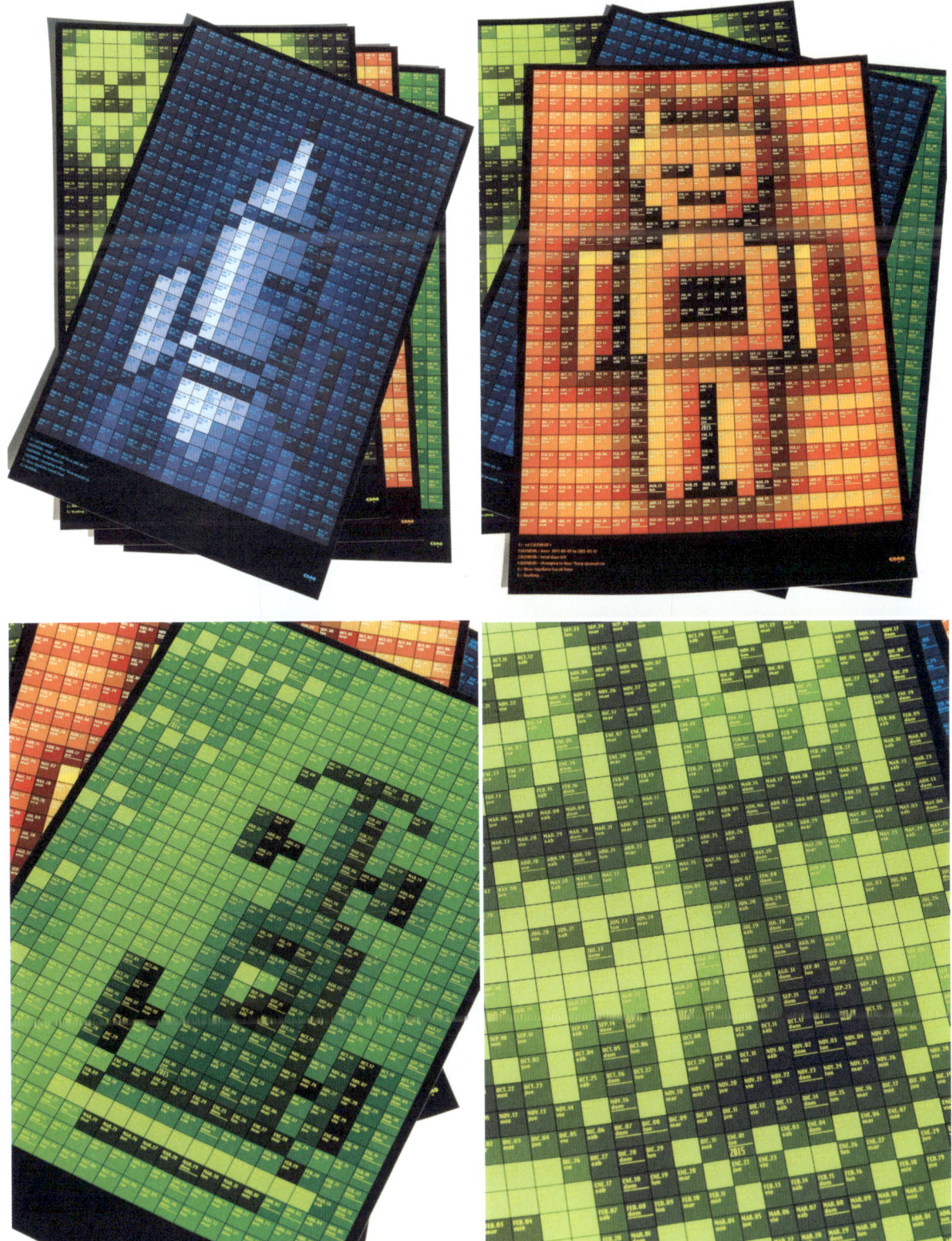

APR
1

April Fools Day

2014 Desktop Calendar for ANTALIS

Design   Emilija Užukauskiene
Photography Artiom Ištuganov

The main idea of the 2014 ANTALIS desktop calendar was to encourage customers to write letters on paper, send paper cards and to use paper for warm and heartfelt communication.

To implement this idea, envelopes (170×170mm) were used as the basis to print the dates. To tell months apart, different envelopes and various printing techniques were used for each month. All envelopes enclose a post card (150×150mm) created for respective seasonal holidays. Twelve different cards are a gift to a customer encouraging to welcome and cheer his fellows or relatives every month. The postcards were printed on decorative paper, using a variety of printing techniques. Decorative paper and envelopes were selected from the Antalis assortment, not only to implement the idea, but also to promote a range of paper.

Fedrigoni Desk Calendar 2015

Design   Jodie-Ann Langley
Photography   Chris Lineker

Brief: To design a 2015 desk calendar for Fedrigoni customers that promotes their "Woodstock" paper range.

Concept: "Woodstock" is a unique paper range made from 80% recycled pre-consumer waste and 20% FSC certified Virgin fibre. The desk calendar needs to be functional and visually pleasing, whilst promoting this uncoated pulp collection of coloured papers.

Solution: Promoting the naturalness of the "Woodstock" range, the 2015 Fedrigoni desk calendar takes inspiration from where it originates from — the tree. The design is beautifully simplistic so it does not steal attention from the paper range, and to satisfy the designers who will receive the calendar.

APR 5

Cold Food Festival

The Cube Calendar

Design   Stroomberg (Philip Stroomberg)
Printing   Drukgoed&paardekooper
Cardboard IGEPA Nederland

The Cube Calendar adds an innovative twist to the concept of the tear-off calendar. Inspired by thoughts about time, it is a compact object that gradually changes shape: by tearing off a card each day, the user reveals the workings of time.

Divided into six rows, hundreds of cardboard cards line up and are held together as a cube by two binding screws. The cards have been punched from two sheets of cardboard. There's a card for each day, and every few days, there is a card with a quote about time — humorous observations or philosophical aphorisms.

The Cube Calendar comes in a specially designed box that folds around the cube without glue or other adhesive. If you lift the lid, the box falls open like origami, leaving the calendar to be picked up.

Put four boxes side by side, and you'll get the name The Cube Calendar.

APR
7
World Health Day

> Be the change that you wish to see in the world.
> Mahatma Gandhi

Wall Street English Calendar 2014

Design   Luca Fontana

Wall Street English is a global institute for learning English, which gives you the possibility to enhance your English and your future.

The illustrations represent everyday objects and goals that you should follow to improve your English.

Stegosaurus
Paper-craft Calendar

Studio   Digitprop
Design   Markus Fischer
Photography Markus Fische, Digitprop

This cute and whimsical stegosaurus calendar is an easily assembled paper-craft project. The "dinosaur" serves as a holder for 52 cards, each representing one week. The cards have tabs that become the blades of the stegosaurus when inserted into the holder, giving the animal its iconic silhouette. A new set of cards is provided each year as a free printable, so that the actual stegosaurus can be reused.

APR 9 — Day of the Finnish Language (Finland)

Dance Like No One is Watching

Studio The Fingersmith
Design Lin Looi, Sumaya Mahadevan, Ella Zheng, Alicia Wee, Huzaifa Kamal, Raj, Kelyn Lau, Rino Aiigo, Djohan Hanapi, Dawn Ang, Visual Inconsideration

The eleven artists, recruited mostly from a close knitted group of students and recent graduates from LASALLE College of the Arts, faculty of Design Communication were asked to custom design each month according to a theme. In addition to the group of students and recent graduates, a call-to-entry invitation posted on the Fingersmith Letterpress's Facebook page also saw a number of talented artists coming forward to complete the line-up.

The theme chosen was "Dance Like No One is Watching", where each artist interpreted it in their own way. The array of designs received was the underlying reason why the Fingersmith initiated this collaboration. It was a celebration of creative expression — a reminder that everyone should dance to their own tune and that life is too short to worry about what other people think. Besides, this project was a way to showcase the multitude of illustration talents on this puny island. It was a platform for people to come together to do stuff and just have fun.

100 pieces of calendars were letterpressed with Klaus, our 54-year-old Heidelberg Windmill, producing a tactile feel to all the designs. The calendar was given out to artists and guests at the Fingersmith Letterpress's private Christmas party to ring in the good tidings.

Calendar 2014

Studio   Reboot Creative Agency
Design   Katerina Mahaira

Butterfly 2014 Calendar was created in two versions: portrait & landscape.

We used straight lines to represent the course of weeks & months, that are "interrupted" and full of circles — an ideal shape — one for each day.

We absolutely love butterflies, as well as their symbolism. Inspired by the theory that a single wing flap can change the course of everything, we added them to every month. Filled with specific colors to represent specific days, the butterflies' tones & shades gave our calendar a more playful and sweet feeling to the rather geometrical design, which we hoped everyone would enjoy.

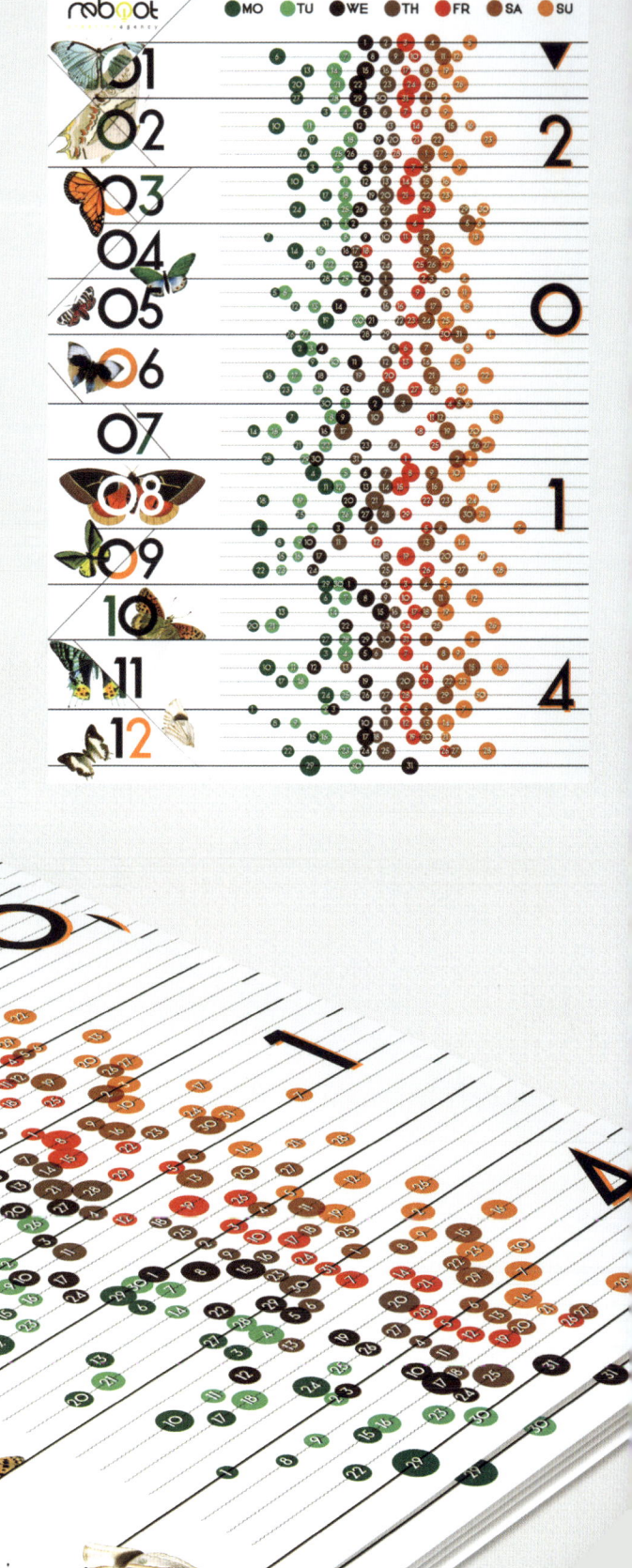

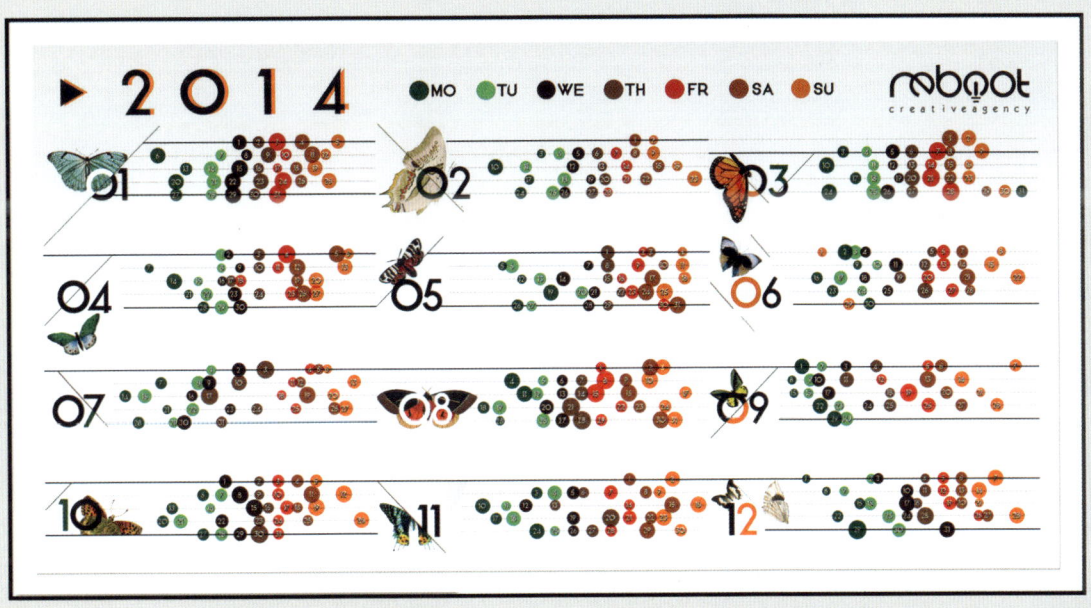

APR 13

Undiagnosed Children's Awareness Day

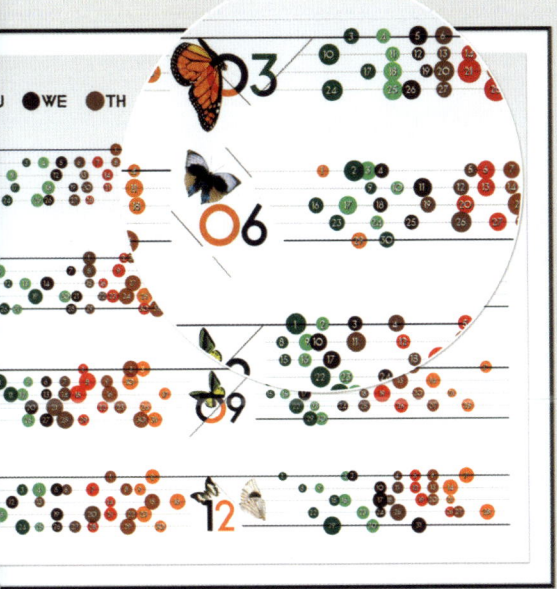
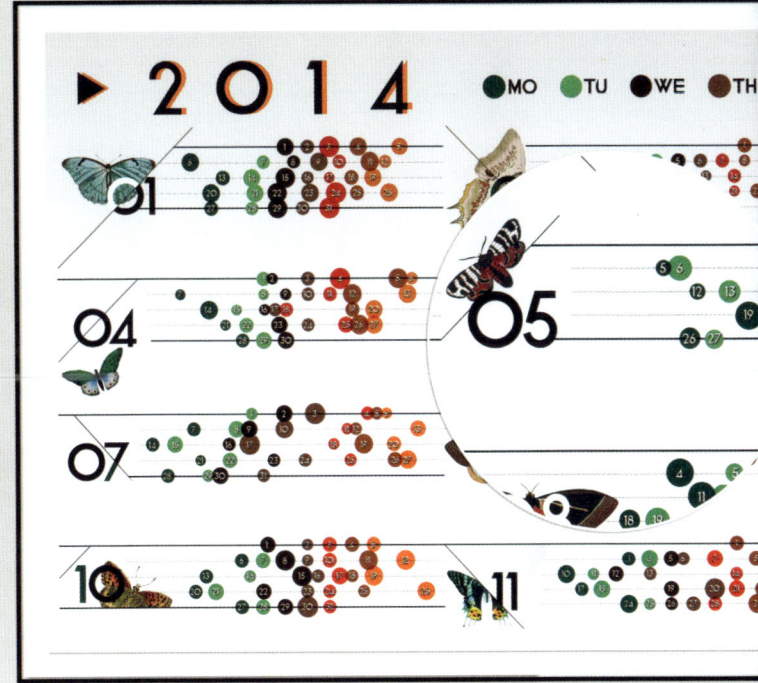

Natural (2014 Calendar)

Design Ainorwei Lin

A Gipsy legend that says that humans are born with "colour natures" according to the seasons and the changes of Mother Nature when a person was born. The calendar utilized symbolic figures and colours to represent the meaning of every month based on these "colour natures".

APR
15

Day of Silence

2012 Calendar

Design   LO SIENTO

A 2012 Calendar made by LO SIENTO to give as a gift. Each of the polyhedrons has different number of faces, corresponding with the number of each month.

APR
17

World Hemophilia Day

Illustrative Calendar 2014

Studio Bel's Art World
Design Belinda Chen

These mischievous, funny and cut-out little characters can be displayed happily on your walk or desk, to cheer you up every single day. The 12 illustrations are printed on ecological natural recycled card, using silk screens with 5 different colours.

APR 19 — Bicycle Day

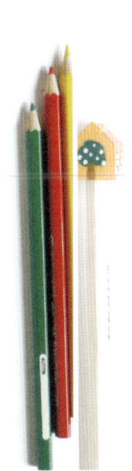

Jan 2014

S	M	T	W	T	F	S
			1	2	3	4
5	6	7	8	9	10	11
12	13	14	15	16	17	18
19	20	21	22	23	24	25
26	27	28	29	30	31	

Feb 2014

S	M	T	W	T	F	S
						1
2	3	4	5	6	7	8
9	10	11	12	13	14	15
16	17	18	19	20	21	22
23	24	25	26	27		

Mar 2014

S	M	T	W	T	F	S
						1
2	3	4	5	6	7	8
9	10	11	12	13	14	15
16	17	18	19	20	21	22
23	24	25	26	27	28	29
30	31					

Apr 2014

S	M	T	W	T	F	S
		1	2	3	4	5
6	7	8	9	10	11	12
13	14	15	16	17	18	19
20	21	22	23	24	25	26
27	28	29	30			

May 2014

S	M	T	W	T	F	S
				1	2	3
4	5	6	7	8	9	10
11	12	13	14	15	16	17
18	19	20	21	22	23	24
25	26	27	28	29	30	31

Jun 2014

S	M	T	W	T	F	S
1	2	3	4	5	6	7
8	9	10	11	12	13	14
15	16	17	18	19	20	21
22	23	24	25	26	27	28
29	30					

APR
21

Vietnam Book Day (Vietnam)

Jul 2014

S	M	T	W	T	F	S
		1	2	3	4	5
6	7	8	9	10	11	12
13	14	15	16	17	18	19
20	21	22	23	24	25	26
27	28	29	30	31		

Aug 2014

S	M	T	W	T	F	S
					1	2
3	4	5	6	7	8	9
10	11	12	13	14	15	16
17	18	19	20	21	22	23
24	25	26	27	28	29	30
31						

Sep 2014

S	M	T	W	T	F	S
	1	2	3	4	5	6
7	8	9	10	11	12	13
14	15	16	17	18	19	20
21	22	23	24	25	26	27
28	29	30				

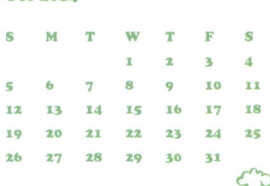

Oct 2014

S	M	T	W	T	F	S
			1	2	3	4
5	6	7	8	9	10	11
12	13	14	15	16	17	18
19	20	21	22	23	24	25
26	27	28	29	30	31	

Nov 2014

S	M	T	W	T	F	S
						1
2	3	4	5	6	7	8
9	10	11	12	13	14	15
16	17	18	19	20	21	22
23	24	25	26	27	28	29
30						

Dec 2014

S	M	T	W	T	F	S
	1	2	3	4	5	6
7	8	9	10	11	12	13
14	15	16	17	18	19	20
21	22	23	24	25	26	27
28	29	30	31			

Let it Snow

WORLD'S FESTIVALS — ON PAPER

Studio   cyclos design GmbH
Design   Jutta Schnieders, Frank Seepe
Printing   wilke Mediengruppe, GRÄFE Druck & Veredelung GmbH,
              Siebdruck Klein GmbH, moers print + media GmbH
Photography Photographers of their respective countries

According to the theme "WORLD'S FESTIVALS — ON PAPER", Europe's major paper and packaging group Antalis invites you to experience spectacular international festivals on a round-the-world trip on paper.

Cyclos design created a unique calendar which paid a creative tribute to twelve festive days and celebrated a colourful cascade of festivals in a multifaceted way. Every single calendar sheet consists of a premium paper with special characteristics that make you "feel" the festivals, for example, the Chinese ice and snow festival is printed on paper with sparkling particles that reflect the light like ice. Moreover, each festive day has its own visual language, with special pictogram and elaborated print finishings matching the characteristics of the festival, like the fluorescent colours that represent the illuminated lanterns on the night of Buddha's birthday. A highlight is a small high-quality information brochure on each calendar page providing interesting details on the festival depicted.

APR 23 — World Book Day

City Calendar

Design   Shkraba Yekaterina,
                 Ermakov Sergey
Art Direction Shkraba Yekaterina
Illustration   Ermakov Sergey
Photography   Shkraba Yekaterina

Interactive calendar created as a New Year gift for clients of advertising agency Smart Media. The concept of a calendar – a fantastic city, shows the process of the changing weather according to the seasons of the year.

C|M|Y|K Farbfächer Kalender 2014

Design   Peter von Freyhold

This calendar is a daily inspiration for colour lovers. Each day, a colour stripe can be tore off and new colour combinations come up. Printed on coated and uncoated paper, the stripes can be collected to create colour swatches with the use of a bookbinder screw, which is integrated in the head of the calendar. The exact C|M|Y|K data are printed on every stripe.

The calendar contains 371 unique colour stripes, printed on 210 g/m² two sided chromo cardboard from Fedrigoni. The date is printed in silver, and the holidays are white. The German edition is published by Verlag Hermann Schmidt Mainz and was awarded bronze at the Gregor International Calendar Award 2014.

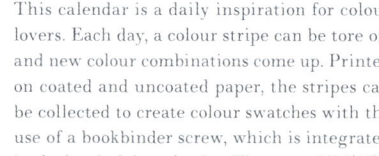

APR
27

Freedom Day (South Africa)

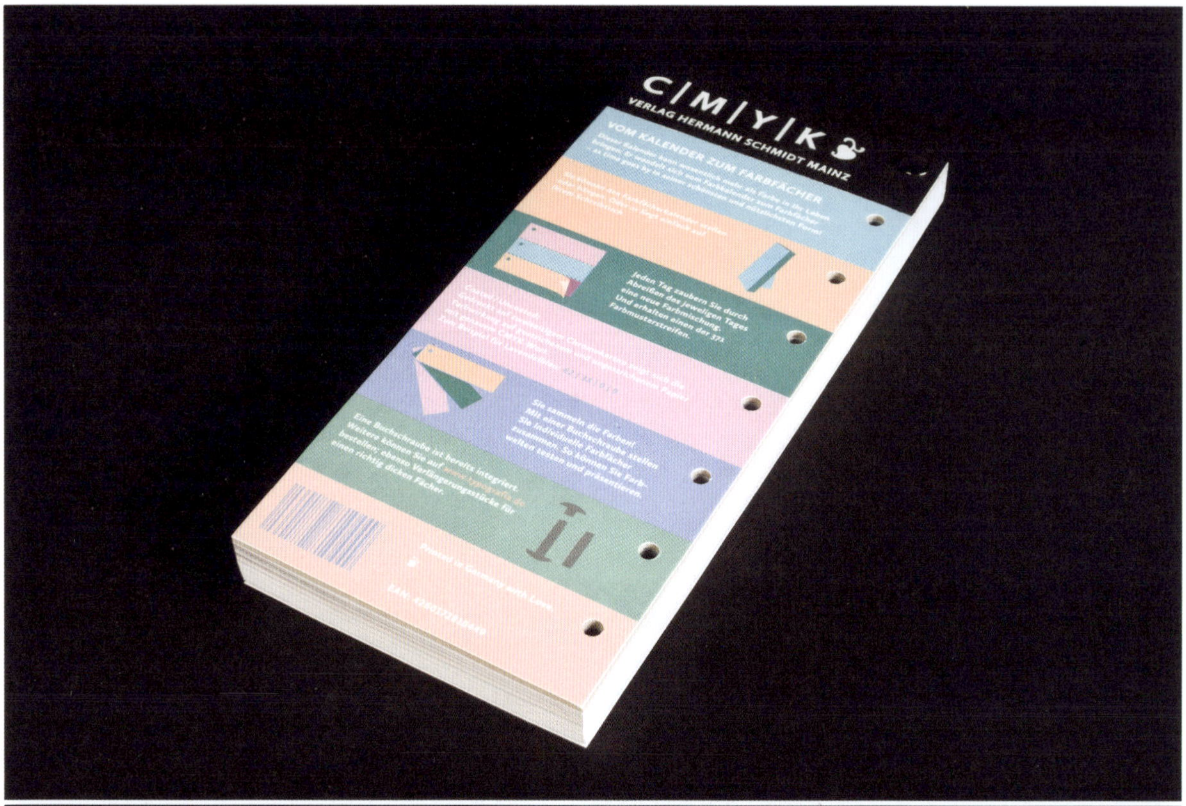

APR 29

International Dance Day

12 Little Monsters

Studio busybuilding
Creative Direction Dimitris Gkazis
Design Konstantinos Trichas
Photography Dimitris Poupalos

"12littlemonsters" is the agency's calendar, designed as a gift for partners and clients for 2011. The edition was produced in collaboration with Perrakis Papers. It is a wall piece designed to unfold bi-monthly and creates a totem of 12 imaginary "monsters".

Due to the financial crisis, 2011 is supposed to be a "monstrous" year for our country. The concept was based on offering a positive perspective for the new year.

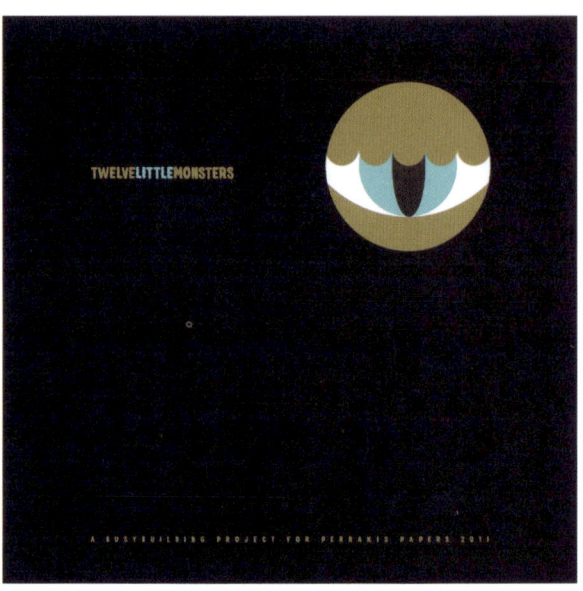

Run Run Run Calendar

Studio BFD Fabian Greiser
Design Fabian Greiser, Tobias Katzenberger

A calendar with silver rub-off paint to document your running activities, keeping track of your running habits during a whole year and helping yourself to stay focused. You can also find important marathon events in Germany as well as all world marathon major dates (WMM) on the calendar for 2014.

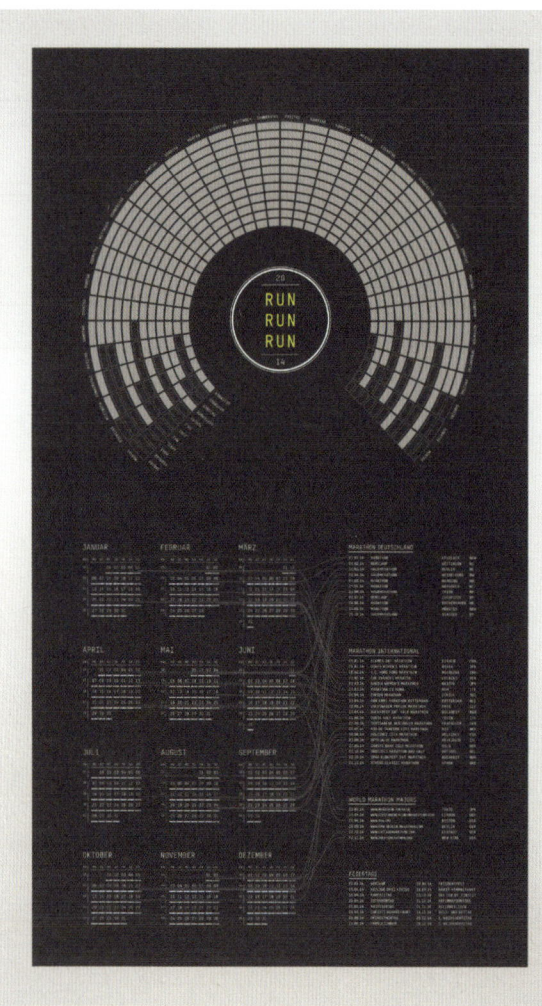
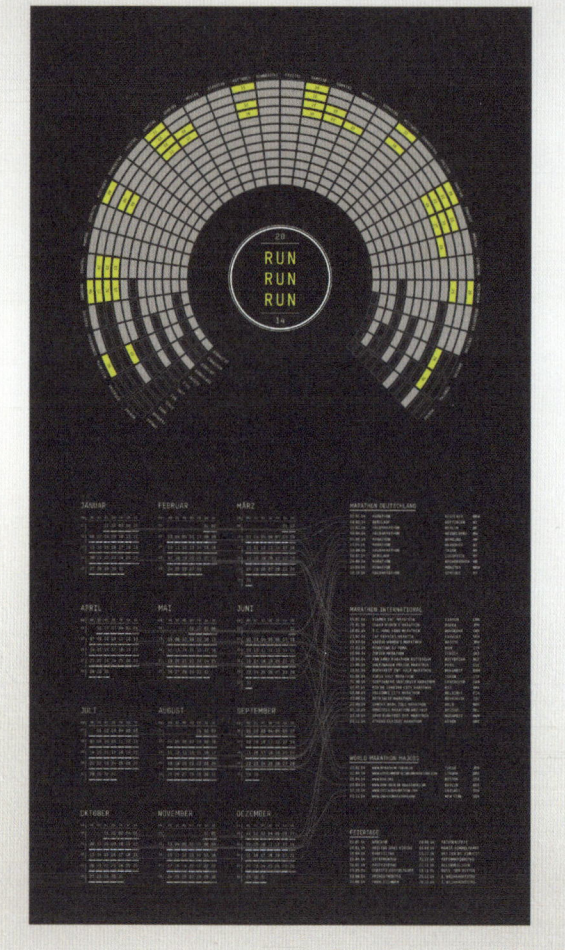

MAY 3

World Press Freedom Day

Star Wars Day

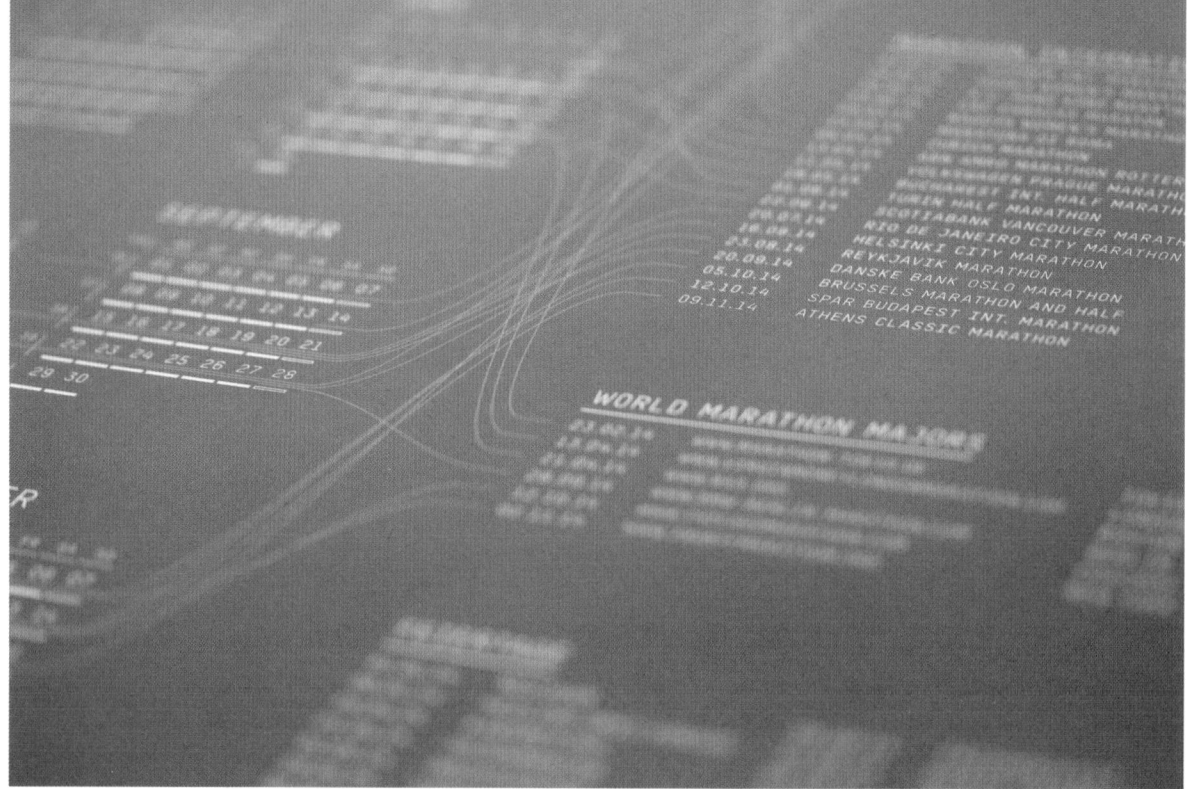

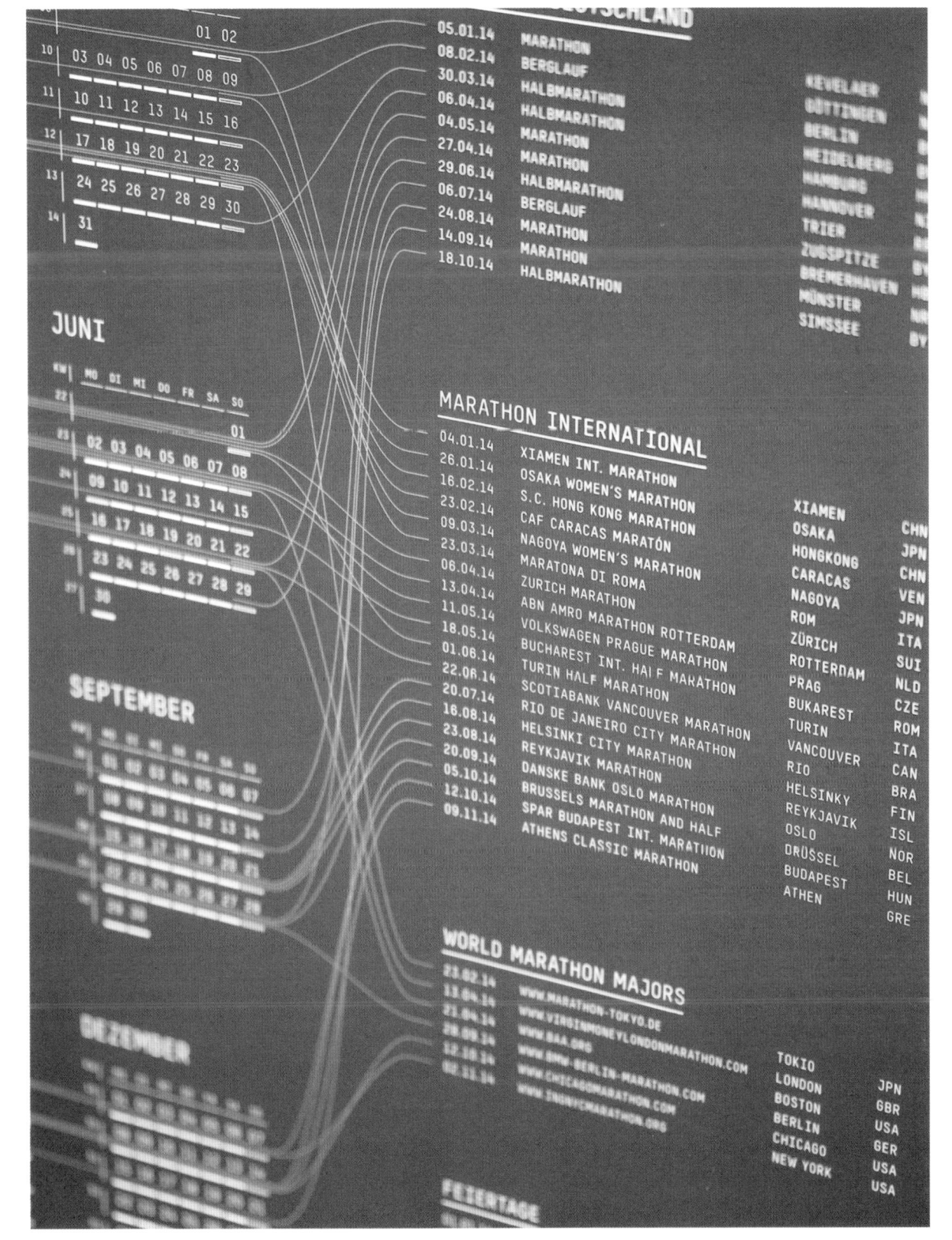

Homeless Monsters Calendar 2012

Design Carlos Higuera

Monsters can exist in fantasies or dreams, they may be fictitious and sometimes real, and can cause fear, awe, admiration and even affection. Monsters inhabit anywhere and can hide under the bed, in the closet, in the basement or up in offices. Yet there are monsters that do not like to remain hidden, are very friendly and enjoy the company of others. The Homeless Monsters 2012 Calendar is full of monsters, because we know you love friends from another world full of colours, with which you can experience thousands of adventures.

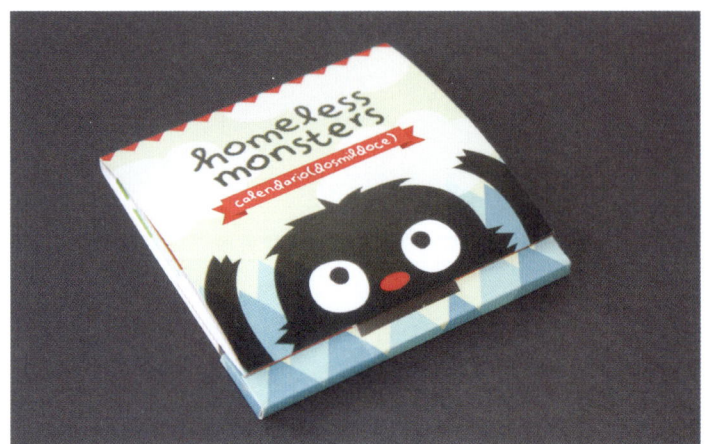

MAY 8
World Red Cross and Red Crescent Day

Los monstruos pueden existir en fantasías o en sueños, pueden ser ficticios y a veces reales, pueden causar miedo, asombro, admiración y hasta ternura. Habitan en cualquier lugar y se esconden debajo de la cama, dentro del armario, en el sótano y hasta en las oficinas.

Sin embargo existen monstruos a los que no les gusta permanecer ocultos, son muy amigables y disfrutan de la compañía, por eso homeless te trae el calendario dosmildoce repleto de monstruos, porque sabemos que te encantan los amigos de otro mundo lleno de colores, con los que podrás vivir miles de aventuras.

   febrero   2012

   abril   2012

   marzo   2012

   agosto   2012

Design Invaders

Studio busybuilding
Creative Direction Dimitris Gkazis
Design Kostis Sotirakos, Vicky Nitsopoulou
Photography busybuilding

A limited edition of 116 copies, the calendar is in principal a means of expression with a very traditional approach to production. Every detail is hand-crafted showing the way busybuilding works.

The creative need behind our calendar was to find a way of offering our partners a glimpse in the mentality of a designer's world. For busybuilding, design should "invade" communication and aesthetic notions.

We designed 12 different characters, one for each month of the year, which we named "design invaders". The recipient of the calendar is invited to freely place the "invader" of their choice on the cover and mark it as important/unimportant documents per month, depending on their design mood. The production of the 116 numbered copies took place in-house in our studio.

Military Spouse Appreciation Day

IC Calendar Design

Design Chiii Design Ltd.

This calendar, "IC Calendar" by Nono Leong, introduces local conditions and customs of Macao via a series of lively and beautiful illustrations. Each month is matched with special illustrations that represent the major festival of the month or significant event happened in Macao.

The "IC Calendar" design tried to associate simple and unique illustrations with the neighbourhoods in Macao, and offered audience an insight into the wonderful community lifestyle in Macao. The showcased design are for calendar years 2006, 2012 and 2013.

Orna Paper Calendar

Studio 3nity
Design Director Joseph Foo
Design Raymond Lai, Cheong Zhi Ying
Photographer Cheong Zhi Ying

The 2013 Ornapaper calendar is a summation of the company's new direction. In order to attract more young talents, Ornapaper is re-branding themselves as an innovative and environmentally accountable company. The calendar uses core materials from their business, and has multiple uses. This is part of a list of communication steps that the company will be using to promote their new brand.

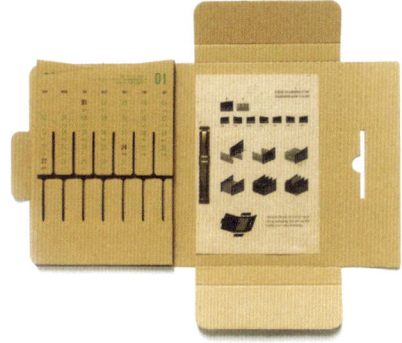

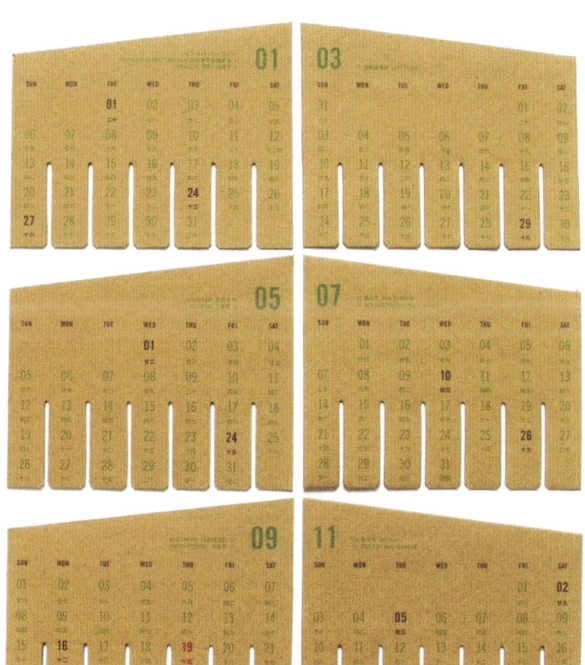

MAY
15

International Day of Families

Seed Calendar

Design Danka Gralik

Seed Calendar is a self initiated project inspired by the work of a designer and activist Amy Franceschini. Since discovering her project, Victory Gardens, I've decided to create my own mini garden kit that serves as a calendar and provides its owner with different seeds suitable for each month of the year. As well as the seeds and care instructions, each month features a short description of Amy's projects to inspire more environmentally friendly behaviour.

Sky Goodies DIY 3D Landscape Calendar

Design   Sky Goodies Products And Applications Private Limited
Photography   The Sky Goodies creative team

A 3D Paper Desktop Calendar for a mantelpiece, table-top or shelf. A multi-layered piece, with quaint little hand-drawn houses, trees and sky! This has been designed as printable Do-it-yourself templates in PDF format.

World Information Society Day

1735km

Design　Tú Bùi

The title of the calendar is "1735km", which is also the distance between Hanoi and Saigon. This calendar is about travelling in Vietnam, showcasing the kind of impression inspired by the journey to six famous and beautiful cities, including Saigon, Dalat, Nha Trang, Hoi An, Hue and Ha Noi.

GREEN CALENDAR

Client   Ohkawa Printing Co., Ltd
Art Direction   Eisuke Tachikawa
Graphic Design   Eisuke Tachikawa,
     Toshiyuki Nakaie
Product Design   Eisuke Tachikawa
Photography   NOSIGNER

We created an original calendar for Okawa Printing, which is a social printing company that emphasizes environment-friendly processes. For this original calendar, we used paper made from thinned wood and environmentally friendly ink. This paper represents wood from trees, which are thinned from Japanese forests in order to protect them. For the base, we also used thinned cedar, to realize a design with low environmental impact. The thinned-wood base is cut diagonally, to allow placement of pens and other small items.

MAY 19 — Hồ Chi Minh's Birthday (Vietnam)

Ciao Calendar

Design Mary McDermott
Photography Mary McDermott

Mary McDermott created Ciao, an English-to-Italian Calendar, where consumers can greet each day by learning a new Italian word. They either see the Italian word first (with an illustration), or the English word first (with a number) and simply lift the tab to reveal the translation. At the end of the month, they can slide off the paper and pop out each perforated day for a memory card. This way, they can play a memory card game to review the words they learned throughout the month before their trip to Italy.

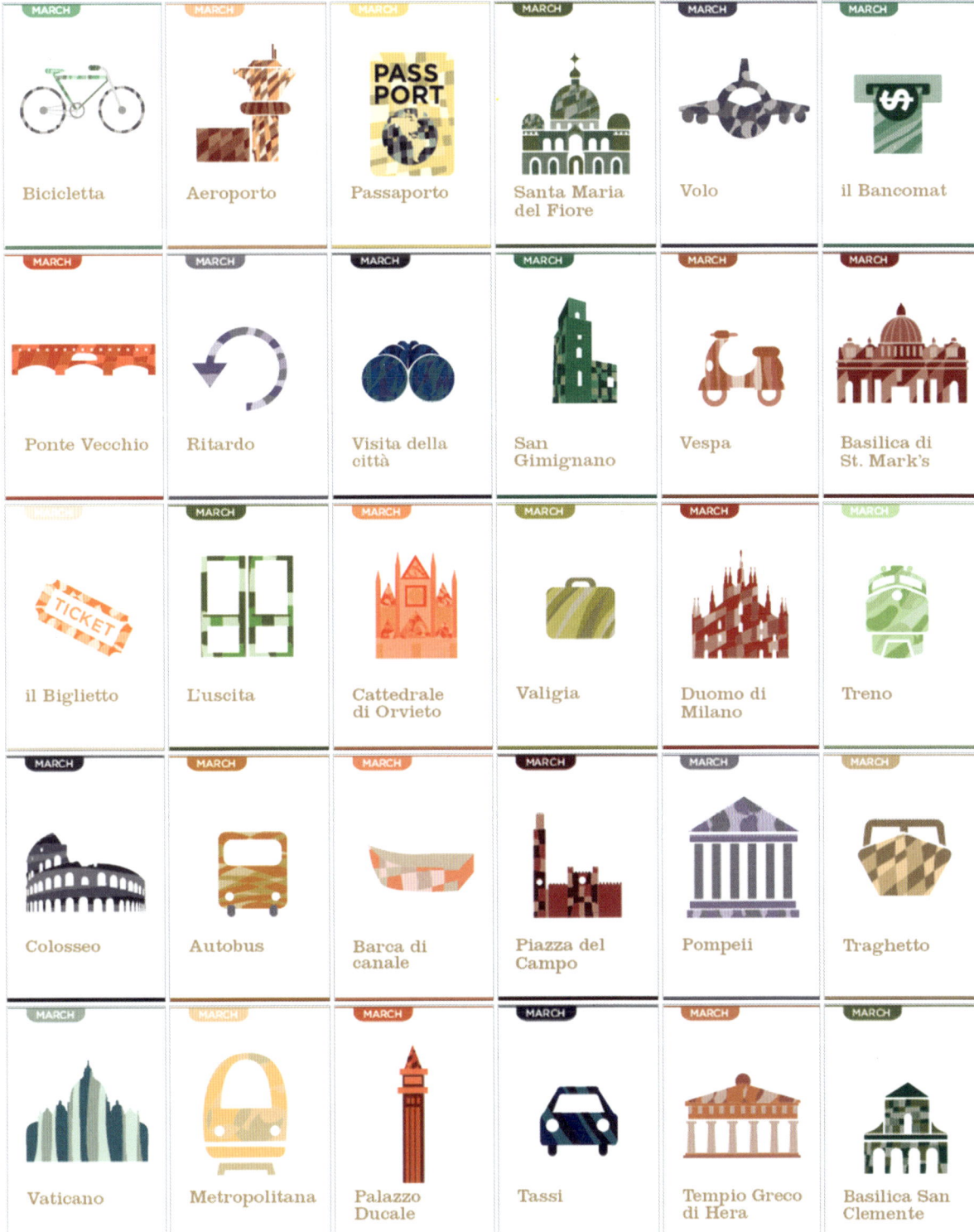

Bit Planner

Studio Special Projects / Vitamins
Design Adrian Westaway,
         Clara Gaggero Westaway
Photography Adrian Westaway

The bit planner is a wall-mounted time planner that we invented for our studio. It's made entirely of Lego, but if you take a photo of it with a smart-phone all of the events and timings will be magically synchronised to an online, digital calendar. It makes the most out of the tangibility of physical objects and the ubiquity of digital platforms, and it also puts a smile on our faces when we use it!

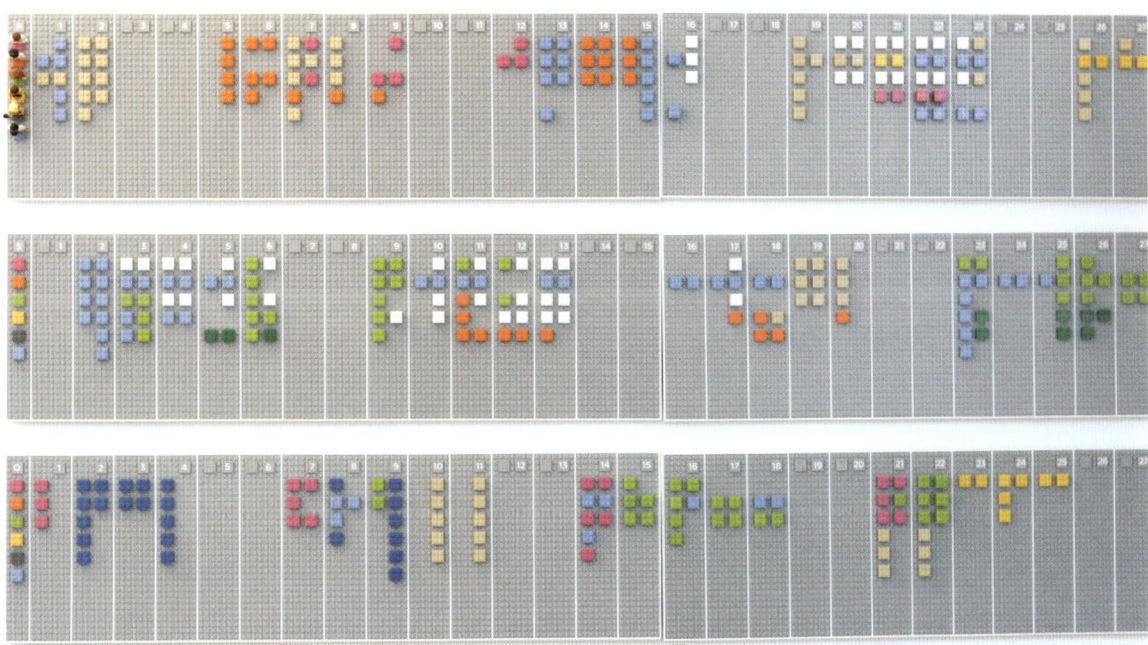

MAY 23

World Turtle Day

Time is Precious

Studio 3EyedBear

Paper-toy calendars for 2014. This bling ring will tell you all there is to know about dates and days, for a whole whopping year long! We believe your boss will gladly allow you to create this cool tool in his time, so he is sure you won't forget what day his birthday is. And watch your girlfriend react when you present it on your knees!

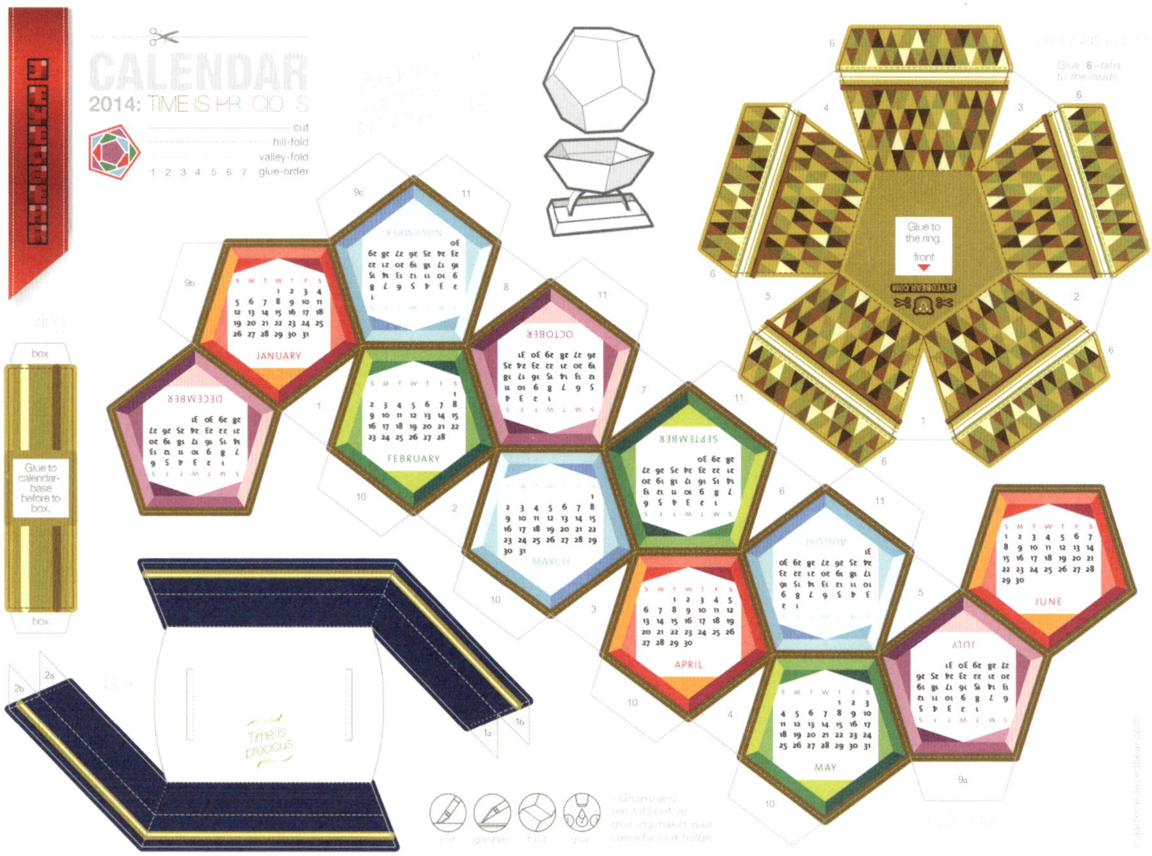

MAY 25

International Missing Children's Day

Sky Goodies Colourful Miniature Typewriter Calendar

Design   Sky Goodies Products And Applications Private Limited
Photography The Sky Goodies creative team

This is a quaint little 3D Paper Desk Calendar for a mantelpiece, table-top or shelf in the form of a vintage typewriter with 12 month cards with dates. The body of the typewriter has been lovingly illustrated with intricate patterns and details, with the graphic style inspired by Indian street art and folk art forms. The calendar combines old-world charm with utility. The calendar is designed as a do-it-yourself template, where the user can assemble. This calendar was featured on Babble.com, thisiscolossal.com, decopeques.com, trendhunter.com and many other portals and blogs.

Slavery Abolition Day (Guadeloupe, Saint Barthélemy, Saint Martin)

Land Rover Topographic Calendar

Agency — TBWA Istanbul
Creative Direction — Ilkay Gürpınar
Creative Group Head — Zeynep Karakasoglu
Art Direction — Zeynep Orbay
Copywriter — Emre Gökdemir

We designed a daily 2014 calendar that reflects the off-road spirit of Land Rover by creating a 3D version of classical, flat topographic maps. Colours on each level represent different months and the numbers on the side of each page show the remaining days of the year.

MAY 29

International Day of UN Peacekeepers

Woodstock is Not: 2015 Desk Calendar for Fedrigoni

Design   Giulia De Rossi,
             Lena Zuern
Photography   Lena Zuern

"Woodstock is Not" is the slogan of this promotional calendar made for a YCN Competition in 2014. The aim was to promote Fedrigoni "Woodstock" paper from a different perspective, showing what Woodstock is not.

Indeed, each month shows a different picture that visualizes the opposite of what "Woodstock" paper is supposed to be, through the use of paper's texture and light. Our aim was to develop and discover a new way of looking at this natural and recycled paper. The minimal typography emphasizes the pictures and the simplicity of "Woodstock" paper. Through the use of folders, the pictures inside can be seen as an additional part, which can be kept or pinned on the wall when the month is over.

The format chosen (125×175mm) is in response to the small space of a desk. Thanks to a rigid support, made by paper as well, the sheets are held without any binding.

JUN
1

International Children's Day

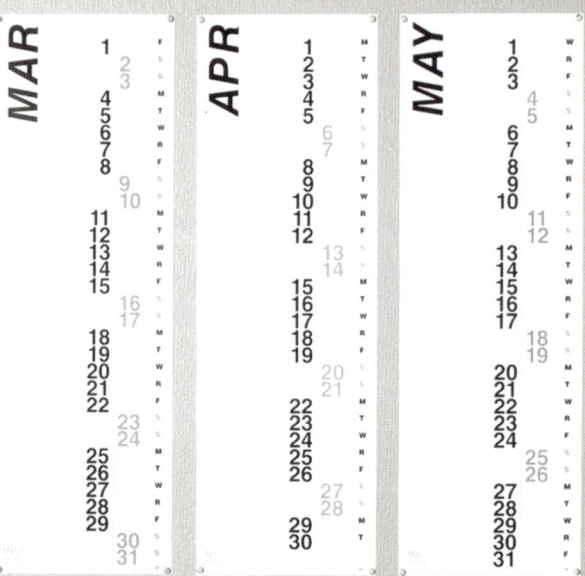

Vertical Calendar

Design MAKE Collaboration

The Vertical is a large wall calendar (12 inches × 36 inches) that displays time in a comfortable, linear fashion. It is set in black Helvetica Neue contrasted on bright white 80# silk book and comes with a hang-up set to eliminate punctures. To us, it is how calendars should be.

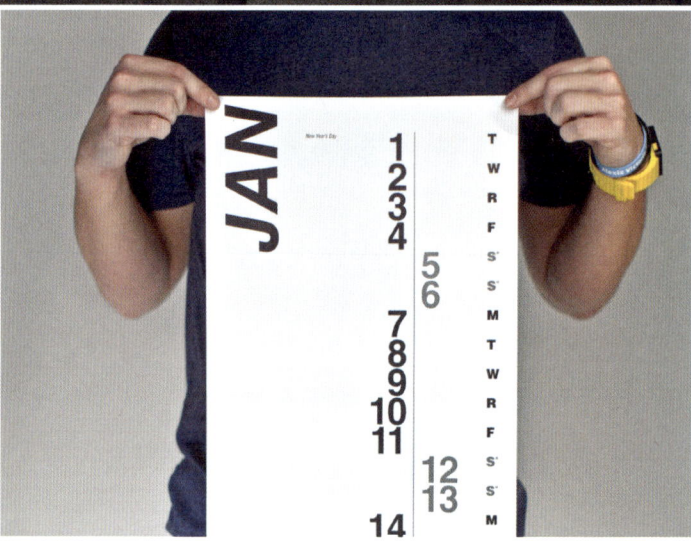

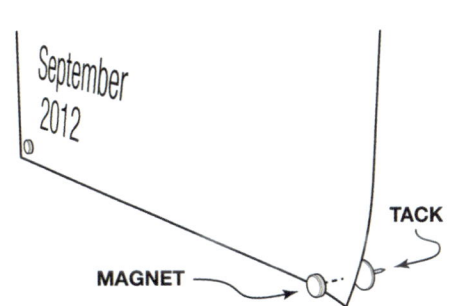

90 Event Stickers

These 90, 3/8" stickers come with each of the Vertical family products, and look even better when they're all together. You know, like a family.

Cup Holder and Calendar

Design   Seoungkyeong Lee
Photography   Seoungkyeong Lee

My challenge is to combine the cup holder and calendar, so that it allows the designer who works on the desk to do two things at once. Apparently, time management is really important for designers but sometimes designers tend to forget to check their schedule. Also, as the quality of "Woodstock" papers by Fedrigoni are absolutely great, the cup holder & calendar is can be used continuously.

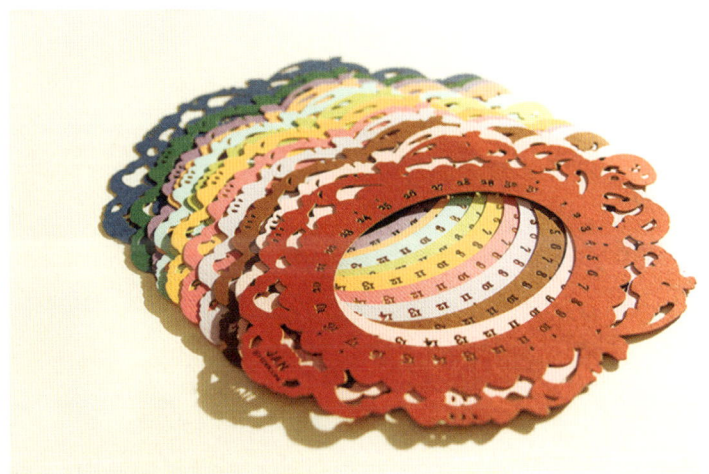

Fedrigoni 2015 Calendar

Design   jihye lee
Photography   jihye lee

Brief: Design a creative functional Desk Calendar for Fedrigoni customers to promote "Woodstock" paper range while maintaining an awareness of the range throughout the 2015.

Solution: Picture frame & mirror calendar. In the office, people usually have a family, friend or lover's picture as well as a small mirror on the desk. The desk is too small for all, so, the 2015 Calendar combines the calendar and the frame as well as the mirror.

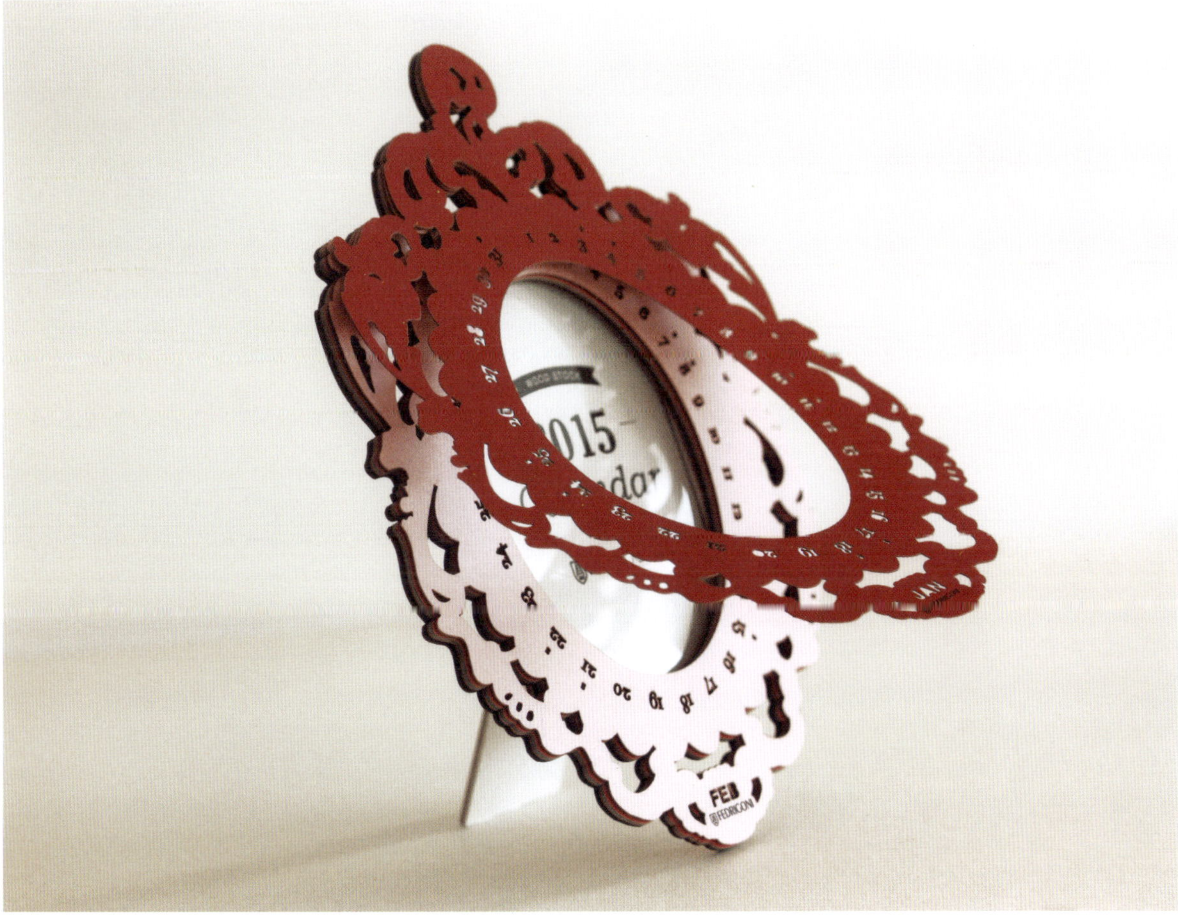

Many Happy Dragons of The Year

Studio Adequate People
Design Elina Zolotareva
Photography Elina Zolotareva

It is typical to give the calendar for the coming year as a New Year present to business partners. The idea was to show the partners that typical and common things can be done in a very different, outstanding and joyful way.

The calendar itself appears to be a set of six dragons (the symbol of the year 2012 was dragon in accordance to Chinese Year Symbols) and a base of two "legs". The calendar also features these dragons based on the seasons and events happening on the month. For example, in Russia, children go to school on the first day of September, so a September dragon holds a book; in March, Women's Day is widely celebrated all over the country, so the dragon carries flowers.

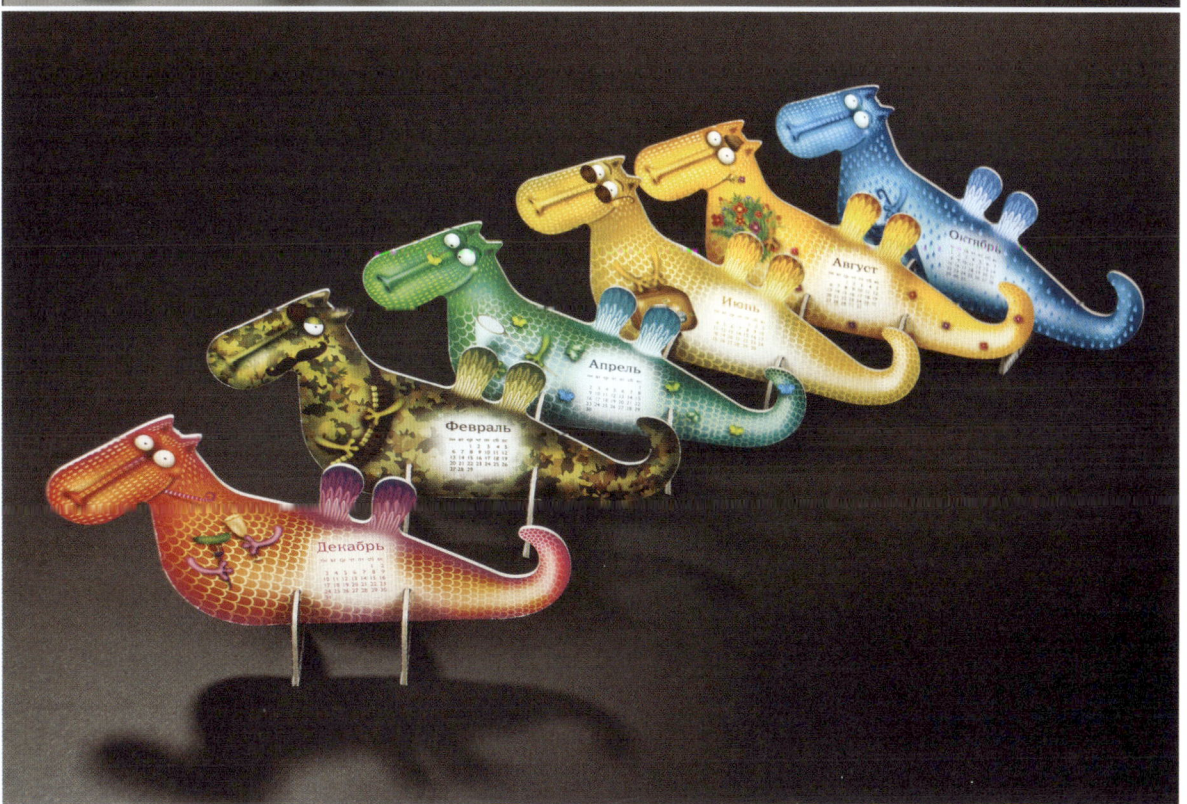

2014 Studio On Fire Desk Calendar

Studio Studio On Fire
Illustration Studio On Fire, Beeteeth, Lab Partners, Brian Gunderson, Jolby, Kate Bingaman-Burt

Each year, we here at Studio On Fire select ink colours, paper stocks, and come up with a theme before asking a slew of illustrators to join us in creating custom artwork for each month. This year we tackled January and October, while the remaining months feature illustrations from the ever talented: Beeteeth, Lab Partners, Brian Gunderson, Jolby, and Kate Bingaman-Burt.

The theme for 2014 was "Happy Place", playing on the concept that your happy place might be an actual place or maybe just something small in your life that brings you joy. From kittens to castles and coffee to burgers, this year is chock-full of delightful illustrations to keep you in a good mood all year (small disclaimer: you might get very hungry in some months).

National Heroes' Day (Uganda)

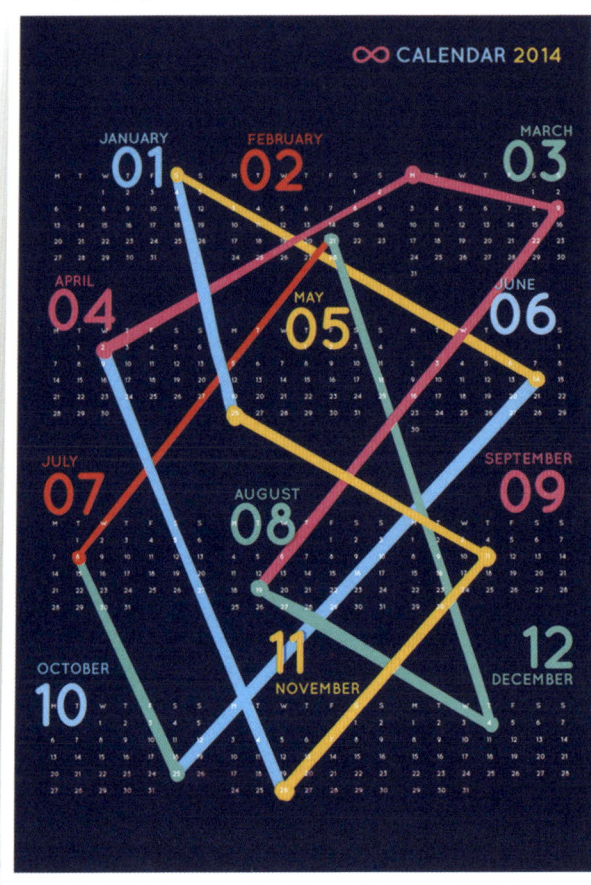

Calendar 2014

Design   Judy Kaufmann

Linked by random days, this colourful calendar is perfect for anyone who wants to have organized days of happiness.

2013 Wall Calendar: Succulent Paper Cut Poster

Studio   CuriousDoodles
Design   Laura Trimell
Laser Cutting   Darrell Rossman

This poster calendar is screen-printed by hand with silver ink then laser cut with a succulent pattern.

JUN 10

Portugal Day (Portugal)

JUN 11

Kamehameha Day (Hawaii, United States)

Calendar EGGHEAD 2013

Design   EGGHEAD
Collaboration   Josephine Tan
Photography   Adam Mulyadi

This year, we have a privilege to collaborate with some of top Indonesia's Printing Companies such as, SUBUR MITRA GRAFISTAMA, PAPER GALLERY, SAMAFITRO, PT PENTAMAPAN CEMERLANG. Using laser cutting and advanced hand-crafted material from SUBUR, we create limited edition 2013 Calendar for our clients.

2014 Elephant Calendar Tea Towel

Design   Meera Lee Patel

This gorgeous tea towel features the 2014 calendar year and a pair of beautiful Indian elephants. These towels are sewn by hand and packaged beautifully and are perfect for gift-giving. They are lovely kitchen items or look stunning hanging on my wall.

Paustian

Studio Homework
Photography Homework

Calendar design for Paustian Furniture.

Calendarinhos

Design Thais Navarro

Thais Navarro designed this cute calendar and posted on the personal blog — Estudio Sortido. Thais Navarro would like readers to have a beautiful and alternative option to the conventional calendars and, the best part of it all — it is available for free!

Thais Navarro also wanted readers to be involved in craft activities, by cutting and folding the parts to glue. The designs are available in 3 formats: paper box, bookmarks and desktop wallpapers.

For the little boxes, Thais Navarro suggests that people can put their goals and look after it. After four months, if they had any success, put some candies and give to somebody they love.

JUN 16

International Day of the African Child

Craft&Tech 2013 Calendar

Studio PaulaMastra
Creative Direction Paula Mastrangelo
Artist Rosa Baldrich,
Marta Solà,
Paula Mastrangelo

I have resorted to the memory of my grandmother Catalina to create all these "work" she taught me to make with my own hands for the 2013 calendar. This calendar was born as a wallpaper and I wanted to show how well it fits technology and craftsmanship.

JUN 18

Autistic Pride Day

170

Memo Calendar

Design   Milk Design Ltd.

A multifunctional calendar with a memo stand that enables users to plan their schedule in a more convenient way. Also, it can still be a practical desktop product after 2014.

There are four colour versions, using fine coloured paper from SKIN CURIOUS Collection and one eco version using waste paper collected from Antalis (HK).

The set comes with a memo pad set suitable for inserting into the paper block. Dates are marked on the top of the wooden structure, and are easy to cross-check with the rotatable monthly calendar printed at the front. It helps to plan your schedule easily by just inserting all your daily memos, business cards, tickets, receipts or important notes into the paper block according to the date markings.

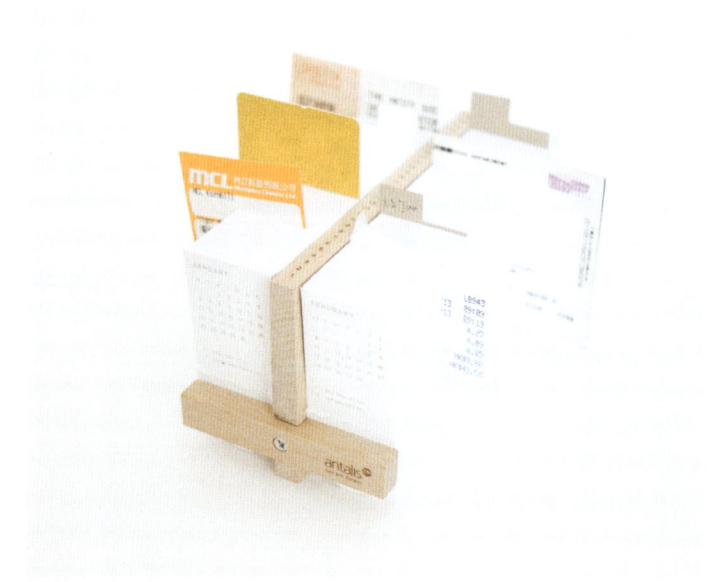

JUN 20

World Refugee Day

Calendar Transformer Kit 2014

Design Margarita Kurtser

Calendar Transformer Kit is my student project. It consists of 12 colour square cardboard modules which can be combined and interconnected in different ways. All numbers and letters are hand printed. Calendar Transformer is interactive object and people can use it as interior decorations, or it can be a good toy for their children.

JUN 22

Anti-Fascist Struggle Day (Croatia)

JUN 23

International Widow's Day

AUTUMN

JUN 24

World Young Doctors' Day

2000+12 Calendar

Studio   Grey Worldwide Jakarta
ECD   Randy Rinaldi
Creative Group Head   Nicholas Kosasih
Senior Graphic Designer   Irene Saputra
Graphic Designer   Kevin Reinaldo, Aditya Pratama
Copywriter   Andika Pandjaitan

KUMON is the world's largest after-school math enrichment program for kids, with 16 million children enrolled in more than 26,000 KUMON Centres in 46 countries, famous for their everyday learning method to optimize children's true potential. As routines can be boring, especially when it comes to education, we wondered how can we introduce the KUMON everyday learning method in a fun and exciting way? The idea: We create a daily fun math calendar that were sent out to families with 5-6 year old children living around KUMON's main branches in the city of Jakarta. As a result, more parents in each neighbourhood come to register their child.

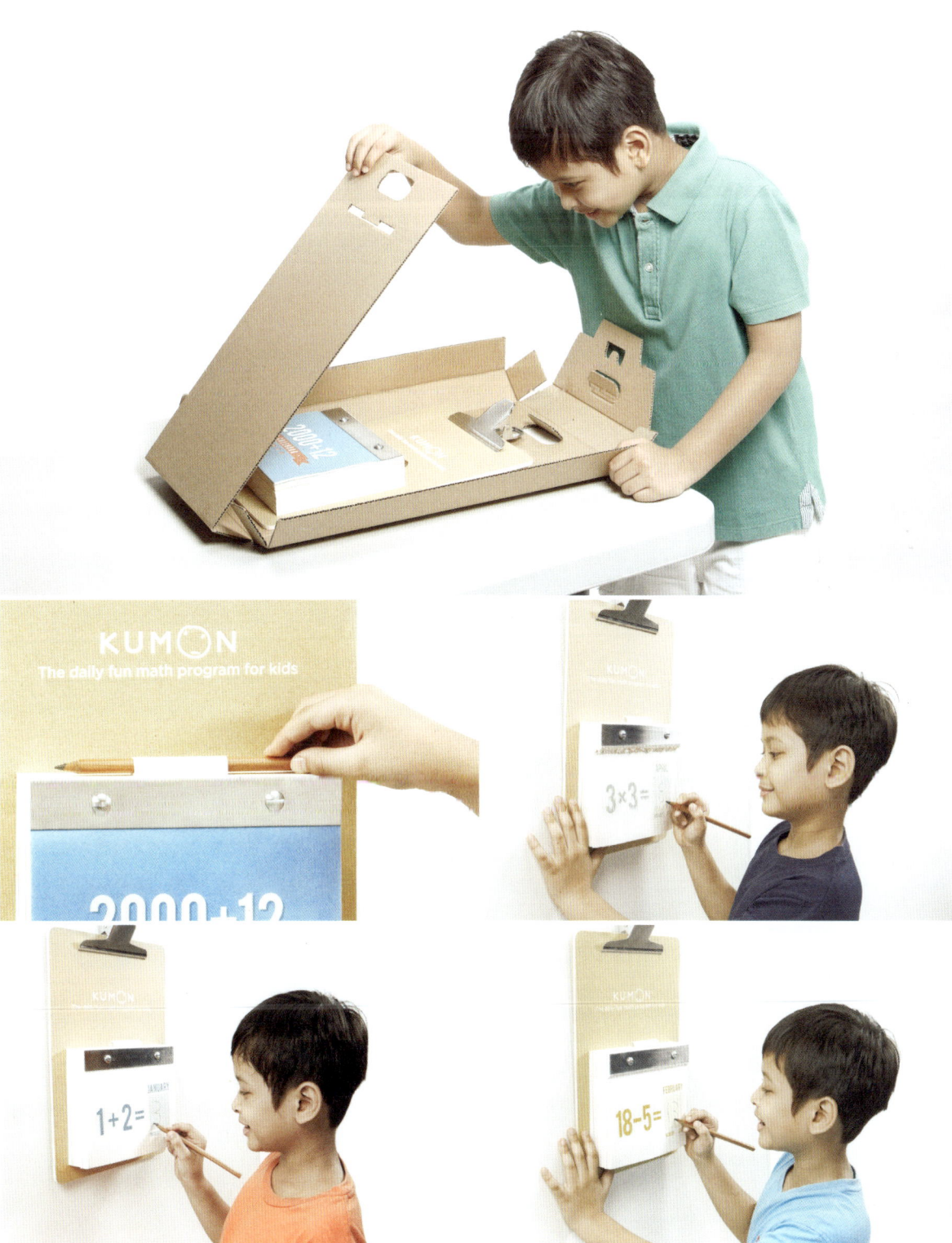

International Day against Drug Abuse and Illicit Trafficking

No Matter How Many Skies Have Fallen

Studio busybuilding
Creative Direction Dimitris Gkazis
Design Tassos Papaioannou
Photography Dimitris Poupalos

Yard is a niche production company specializing in events. Their 2013 do-it-yourself calendar allows users to define each day's creative space themselves, placing specially designed date-stickers wherever they want. In this way, each calendar is not only fully customisable, but a tool of documenting each day's ideas in a non-linear and uniform way, exactly the way profound creativity really works.

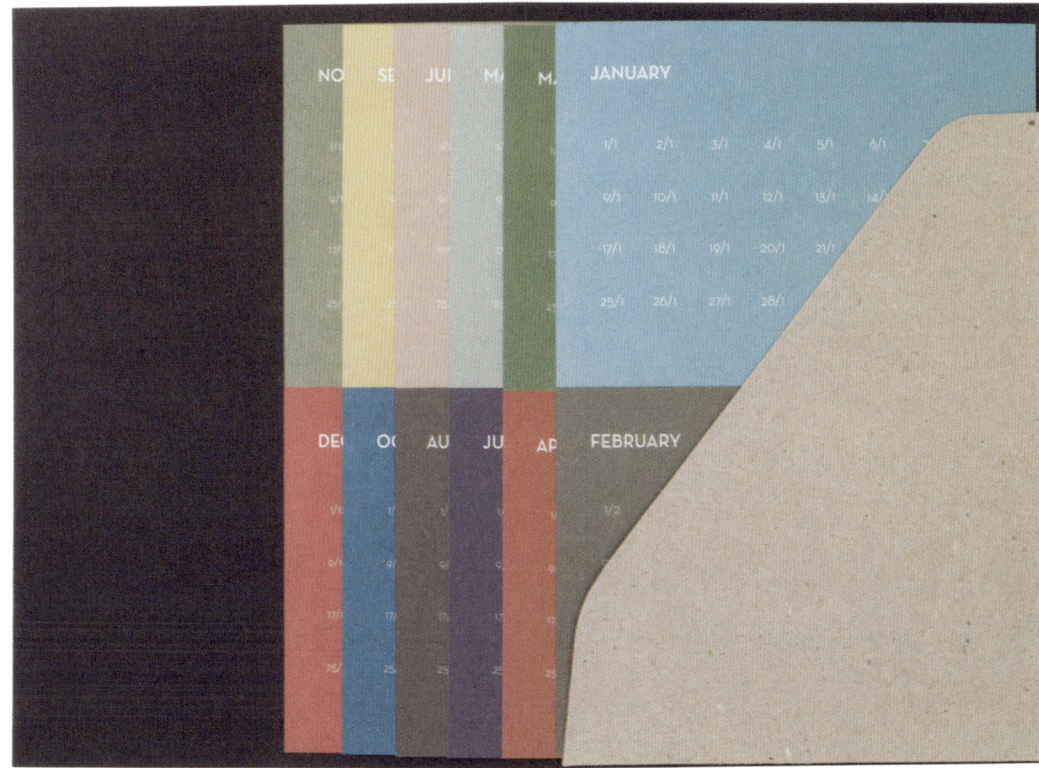

JUN
28

Family Day (Vietnam)

Event Matching System Diary

Design Qube Studio (Singapore)

Today, calendars are not just tools that tell you what day or month it is, but serve a much more subtle role in our lives. A well-designed and aesthetically pleasing calendar can alter the visual aspect of a room and can even be a subject around which casual conversation can revolve.

In our minds a calendar plays an imperative role in our lives and defines us by our tastes and styles. Latest advancements in technology have made it possible for us to incorporate our schedules and events into calendars in a virtual form in our mobile devices and computers, but nothing beats the experience of owning a conventional calendar. There are many who prefer to own and use calendars that are physically present which they can touch and feel, an experience that cannot be replicated by modern technology.

For 2013's Qube Diary, we decided to add a bit of colour and discovered some of the more wacky, frivolous and downright silly events in 2013. EMS refers to "Event Matching System" and for the user to mark the date, we supplied a clever little peel-off swatch sticker for them to remember.

JUN 30

Philippine–Spanish Friendship Day (Philippines)

The Creative Manifesto

Design Fabien Barral
Printing www.elcalotipo.com
Photography Fabien Barral

After the success of the 2011 and 2012 editions of "letterpress calendar", Fabien Barral (Mr Cup) did not schedule one in 2013 as he moved to Bali for a year to work on wood products with local craftsmen (including a collection of Helvetica Alphabet that comes in three different wood).

Back in France, he is associated with the Spanish El calotipo printing studio for the 2014 calendar. Called "The Creative Manifesto", this edition presents creative words of wisdom for every month of the year. Limited to 500 hand numbered copies, it is composed of 13 cards printed on 700g paper plane white frost. Each of the 20×14 cm card has its own colour, referring to the season.

The first 100 copies were sold during the first week of pre-sale and had the distinction of having each card with painted edges. The calendar is only available on the website of Mr Cup www.mr-cup.com and at www.letterpress-calendar.com.

JUL 2

World UFO Day

JUL
3

Women's Day (Myanmar)

Allegheny Financial 2013

Studio Bunch

The 2013 Annual Planner for Allegheny Financial features a bold typographic artwork that was screen-printed in bronze onto a black cloth hard-cover. Since the planner was also given as a gift to their business partners, Bunch designed a paper bag featuring the same artwork.

JUL
4

Independence Day (United States)

Comme une image Calendar

Studio Comme une image
Photography Carla Cascales Alimbau

Every month is accompanied by a handmade illustration inspired in a Haiku, a Japanese short poem, related with the month we are in: seasons, flowers, natural phenomena. The first initial of each month is die-cut so you can see through it. In this case, for the pictures, I chose different flowers related to each season and poem.

JUL
6

Birthday of the 14th Dalai Lama (Tibet)

The Astrozodiac Calendar

Design Corn Studio
Silkscreen Printing Erato & Tind
Label Design Vassia Kalozoumi

The design is based on Josef Manes's calendar, located under Prague's Astronomical Clock, that depicts the 12 zodiac signs alongside rural life scenes from Prague. Each scene in the calendar can be related to the agricultural tasks that took place in that particular month in Prague.

The Astrozodiac Calendar features a redesign of the 12 zodiac signs, alongside illustrations that portray scenes from ancient Greek mythology and mythological creatures, in contrast to Mones's scenes of rural life. The illustrations are based on myths about Gods, heroes and monsters, which were given to each constellation by the ancient Greeks along with their names.

Next to the numbering in his calendar, Manes noted the Saints' holidays. In the Astrozodiac Calendar the numbering is replaced by the moon's phases for the year 2014. Manes used Prague's Castle as the main element for his calendar composition, whereas in the Astrozodiac Calendar this has been replaced by the Sun, quite suitable, considering that the position of the celestial body of the Sun on someone's day of birth, is what defines that person's zodiac sign. The Sun's design is based on the Ancient Greek drama masks, aligned with the design style of the mythological scenes. Located at the bottom of each poster is a summary for each zodiac sign myth, as described by the ancient Greeks. The general layout of the Astrozodiac Calendar is designed with art nouveau elements.

THE ASTROZODIAC CALENDAR

JUL
8

Aries
Aries is the 1st sign of the zodiac, represented by a ram. In the myth of the golden fleece, the ram was originally presented to Nephele by Mercury when her husband took a new wife, Ino, who persecuted Nephele's children, Phrixus and Helle. The ram was given to Nephele to her children, in order to escape. The pair had across the sea on the back of the ram. Helle fell off and drowned, giving her name to the Hellespont, while Phrixus arrived safely in Colchis. That's where he sacrificed the ram to Zeus, who placed it in the constellations.

Cancer
Cancer is the 4th sign of the zodiac, represented by a crab. This tale tells of Thetis the sea goddess. The rumour going around town was that any boys that were born of Thetis would grow up to be more imposing than their father was. Thetis was lonely and likeable, however not one god dared come near Thetis long enough to have kids with her. Thetis had to settle and marry a human, Peleus, and gave birth to a mortal son, Achilles. Thetis held Achilles by the heel and doused him in the Styx River to make him immortal. Achilles fate was to become a glorious warrior who died during the Trojan war.

Libra
Libra is the 7th sign of the zodiac and is represented by a scale. This myth talks about Astraea, in Greek mythology. Astraea was daughter of Zeus and Themis. She and her mother were both personifications of justice, though Astraea was also associated with innocence and purity. She is always associated with the Greek goddess of justice, Dike. According to a myth, Astraea abandoned the earth during the Iron Age. Fleeing from the new wickedness of humanity, she ascended to heaven to become the constellation Libra.

Capricorn
Capricorn is the 10th sign of the zodiac, represented by a goat with crooked horns. Capricorn is related with god Paws. He's one of the Satyrs, human-like creatures with the horns and legs of a goat. He was raised by nymphs after his mother, disgusted by his appearance, abandoned him. Pans tended sheep and goats and was a talented musician. His libidinous nature also drove him to go after the nymphs who usually fled in panic at the sight of him. Pans supported Zeus in his battle with Typhon, and in thanks Zeus immortalised him by transforming him into a star constellation.

Taurus
Taurus is the 2nd sign of the zodiac, represented by a bull. The legend says that Zeus fell in love with Europa, daughter of Agenor, the king of Phoenicia. One day while playing at the water's edge, Europa's attention was caught by a majestic white bull. Zeus in animal form. The bull knelt before her and she climbed upon its back. The bull then flew over the sea towards Crete, where Zeus made Europa his mistress. Europa gave birth to three children, Minos, Rhadamanthys and Sarpedon. Minos became king of Crete and his queen, Pasiphaë, gave birth to a bull-headed son called the Minotaur, who was later slain by Theseus in the Labyrinth.

Leo
Leo is the 5th sign of the zodiac, represented by a lion. The first on the list of Hercules' labours was the task of killing the Nemean Lion, giant beast that roamed the hills of the Peloponnesian villages causing terror. Hercules' arrows bounced harmlessly off of the lion's body, his sword bent in two and his wooden club smashed to pieces. Hercules had to wrestle the beast, ultimately choking it to death. Hercules then wrapped the pelt of the lion around his body to protect himself from his second labor, killing the poisonous sea serpent Hydra. The lion found its way to the heavens to commemorate the great battle with Hercules.

Scorpio
Scorpio is the 8th sign of the zodiac, represented by a scorpion. According to the myth, Orion boasted to goddess Artemis and her mother, Leto, that he'd kill every animal on earth. Although Artemis was known to be a hunter herself, she offered protection to all creatures. Artemis and her mother Leto sent a scorpion to deal with Orion. The pair battled and the scorpion killed Orion. However, the fight was so impressive that caught the attention of Zeus, who later raised the scorpion to heavens and afterwards, at the request of Artemis, did the same for Orion to serve as a reminder for mortals to curb their excessive pride.

Aquarius
Aquarius is the 11th sign of the zodiac, represented by a pitcher of water. In greek mythology Aquarius is identified with Ganymedes, a young man who was spotted by Zeus, who immediately decided that he would make a perfect cup-bearer. Ganymedes was a divine hero whose homeland was Troy. Zeus with his eagle, carried Ganymedes to Olympus mountain to be the cup-bearer of the gods. Ganymedes was the pourer of waters during the mythical great flood, via the Eridanus river.

Gemini
Gemini is the 3rd sign of the zodiac, represented by two twin kids. They share the same mother, Leda, but have different fathers. Castor's father is Tyndareus, the king of Sparta, and Pollux's father is the god Zeus. Pollux is immortal while his twin brother Castor is mortal. Having spent their whole lives together, Pollux was distraught when Castor, being mortal, died. Pollux begged his father for help. Zeus decided to allow the brothers to remain together in a slightly different way. Mortal Castor was allowed to share in Pollux's immortality and eternal life, but immortal Pollux in turn, would also have to share in Castor's mortality and death.

Virgo
Virgo is the 6th sign of the zodiac, represented by wheat. Virgo is associated with the greek goddess Demeter, mother of Persephone. Hades, god of the underworld, promised that he'd make Persephone his queen. Demeter wouldn't allow Hades to marry her so he kidnapped Persephone to the Underworld. During her quest to feed Persephone, Demeter went without food and being the goddess of the Earth this made the land barren. Zeus asked Hades to release Persephone, but she said that she loved her husband Hades. Zeus resolved the conflict by allowing Persephone to spend wintertime in the Underworld and summertime on Olympus.

Sagittarius
Sagittarius is the 9th sign of the zodiac, represented by a bow and an arrow. This myth talks about centaur Chiron. He was king of Centaurs, half man and half horse, who lived with his own tribe among the wild hills and forests of Thrace. He was renowned because of the wisdom he had of life, nature and human behaviour. Chiron was the sage, the teacher, the philosopher. During her quest to feed Persephone, one of the twins about Chiron relates that he received a wound from a poisoned arrow. Because of his wisdom, he'd been granted the gift of immortality from gods, but neither could the wound heal, because the poison was from Hydra Lerna.

Pisces
Pisces is the 12th and last sign of the zodiac, represented by two fishes. The greek myth tells how the goddess of love Aphrodite and her son Eros, were turned into fishes when they dove into the sea, in order to escape the wrath of the titan Typhon, during a war between the gods and the titans. They were tied by their tails with a gold thread, so that they may never be lost. The usual imagery of Pisces depict the two fishes head to tail, tied with a tie and like, or looked yin-yang symbol, to emphasise the male and female aspects.

JUL 9

Constitutionalist Revolution Day (São Paulo)

JUL
10

Nikola Tesla Day

TODAY IS A HOLIDAY! COASTER SET

Creative Direction Carol Mcleod Design
Senior Designer Chris Daigneault
Illustration Amy Caracapa-Qubeck

We wanted to spread cheer during the traditional holiday season while creating a lasting impression with our clients and colleagues throughout the new year. Our eternal coaster set was born out of the calendar of lesser-known National Designations. The set includes 12 pulpwood coasters commemorating a unique National Day for each month of the year. Each coaster design lists the month and date specific to the not-so-familiar "holiday" and visually communicates its quirky theme by a simple line drawing rendered with CMD's brand colours — orange and silver — accompanied by an original humorous or thought-provoking message relative to that "holiday". The gift-like package was first mailed during the December holiday season. Then, fun packages were mailed randomly throughout the following year, embellishing and celebrating the peculiar holidays as they occurred — a rubber chicken for Poultry Day on March 19; sunscreen for National Nude Day on July 21; and a set of Count Dracula teeth for Count Your Buttons Day on October 21!

JUL
12

Malala Yousafzai Day

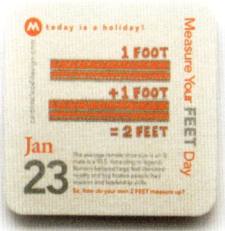

A Box of Elephants

Studio Pop & Zebra
Design Krupa Joshi Desai
Origami Krupa Joshi Desai
Photography Abhishek Desai

"A Box of Elephants" is a limited edition calendar made by Pop & Zebra, to be sent out to their clients. The 2014 annual calendar was designed as a tribute to the African elephants being mindlessly killed for their ivory.

Pop & Zebra invited their Facebook fans to send in their hand drawn elephant illustrations. Out of all the amazing drawings received, 13 were short-listed and used for the calendar. Each illustration was converted to black & white graphics and printed using the risograph technique to keep the production costs low. Special lightweight bespoke wooden boxes were created for these calendars to be sent in. Wrapped in black furoshiki, each calendar is packed with a hand drawn, patterned origami elephant carrying a special note for the receiver.

JUL
14

Republic Day (Iraq)

196

JUL 15

Elderly Men Day (Kiribati)

Gruppo Giovani Industriali Como Calendar

Design   CCRZ
Photography   CCRZ

This calendar for "Unione Industriale di Como" (Como Industry Association) is printed on a synthetic opaline material that allows users to write on it with a pencil or a pen. Every sheet is like a filter so it is possible to see future months through transparent pages.

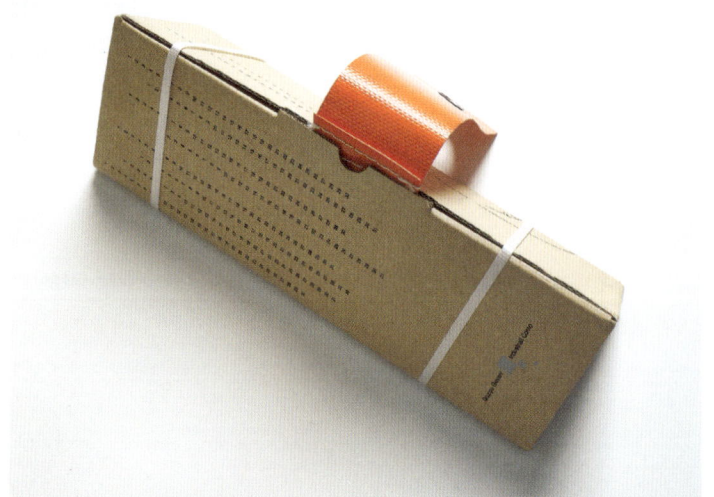

JUL
18

Nelson Mandela International Day

CAreLender 2014

Studio   The Conservancy Association
Design   Benny Lau Siu Tsang
Writing   Katie Chick Hiu Lai, Teresa Tsui Wai Shan
Editing   Betty Lam Lai Shan, Clorie Ng
Photographers   Ching Ho Yin, Teresa Tsui Wai Shan

With similar designs to the 2013 CAreLender, the 2014 edition evolved into a weekly calendar with some variations in content focusing more on local ecology and cultural heritage. The packaging was lighter and more eco-friendly. It was produced locally with FSC paper in soy-ink printing and the binding procedures were completed by local social enterprises. 26 pages of the CAreLender also served as discount coupons to be used in traditional shops, social enterprises and organizations to promote ethical consumption and local green living.

JUL
20

Friend's Day (Argentina, Uruguay, Brazil)

upstruct calendar 2014

Studio upstruct
Design Toni Harzer, Lars Trautmann

A poster in A1 size with 12 beautiful monthly illustrations and a minimalistic calendar. It is a two-colour screen-print (black and neon-orange) on 240g Munken Lynx stock and has an edition of 55 copies.

JUL 22 — Pi Approximation Day

Hua

Studio   FUUFF
Design   Neville Lam, Roy Chan
Photography   Jeffrey Wong @ e5

Hua is a seasonal calendar. Unlike western calendars, Hua begins in spring. Inspired by the cyclical/ephemeral nature of time, Hua is an exploration of forms destroyed and reconstituted to create new ones — much like how death creates new life. The grid of the calendar is based on the layout structure of the traditional Chinese almanacs.

The Chinese typeface was (re)drawn from the parts of a 20-year old Roman typeface. Every detail of the finished piece — from its name, paper stock to cover imagery — was chosen to evoke the transience of time.

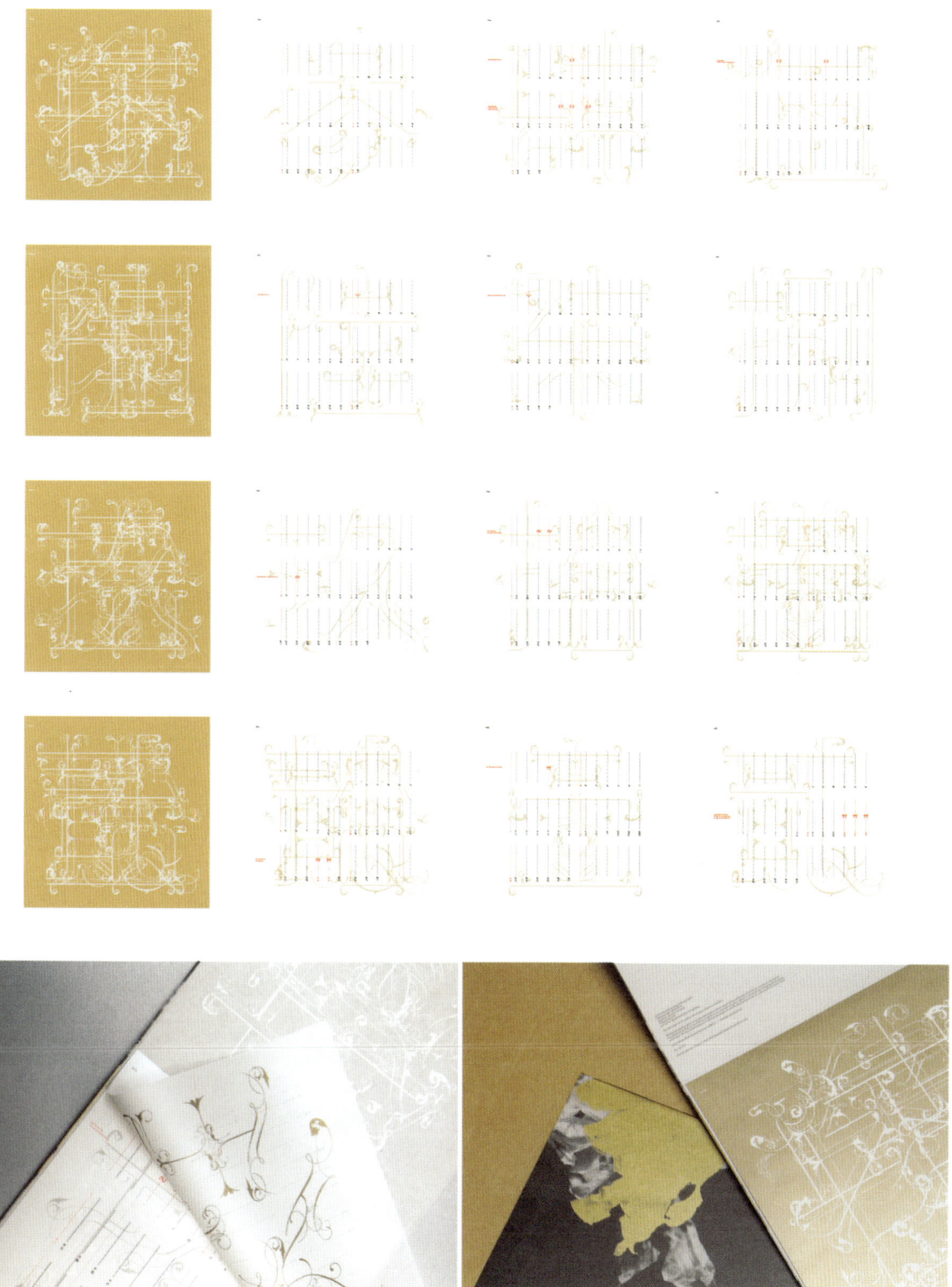

JUL
24

Children's Day (Vanuatu)

Almanac Calender

Design   Daniel Ting Chong
Printing   Essie Letterpress

In collaboration with Essie Letterpress, Daniel Ting Chong was asked to create an illustration for the month January. The illustration depicted the transitional stage of being on holiday and returning to work.

JUL
26

Day of the National Rebellion (Cuba)

daniel ting chong

holiday to monday

JANUARY

T	W	T	F	S	S	M	T	W	T	F	S	S	M	T	W
1	2	3	4	5	6	7	8	9	10	11	12	13	14	15	16
17	18	19	20	21	22	23	24	25	26	27					
				28	29	30	31								

Polytrade Calendar Memo

Design   Eric Chan, Jacky Wong

We took the brief by Polytrade paper for designing their 2013 calendar, however instead of designing an ordinary calendar, it was a perfect opportunity to use our creativity and turn the calendar into a memo pad. This will add value to the calendar, and at the same time, make use of this project as a subtle and ingenious launch of Astrobrights paper range. In this way, this special calendar is multi-functioned and would certainly impress users.

The idea was to link up famous surrealist artist René Magritte and Polytrade Paper's passion towards imagination. They believe imagination is always an essential element of design. Therefore, we came up with a design of hiding the most impactful content under a very plain outlook.

The idea was created by using a plain white cover with a die-cut area of René's signature drawings. While peeking through ordinary images, the colourful paper constructed a spectacular parti-coloured content. This calendar/memo pad will surprise the user and highlights the idea: by using your imagination, there is always something wonderful to explore.

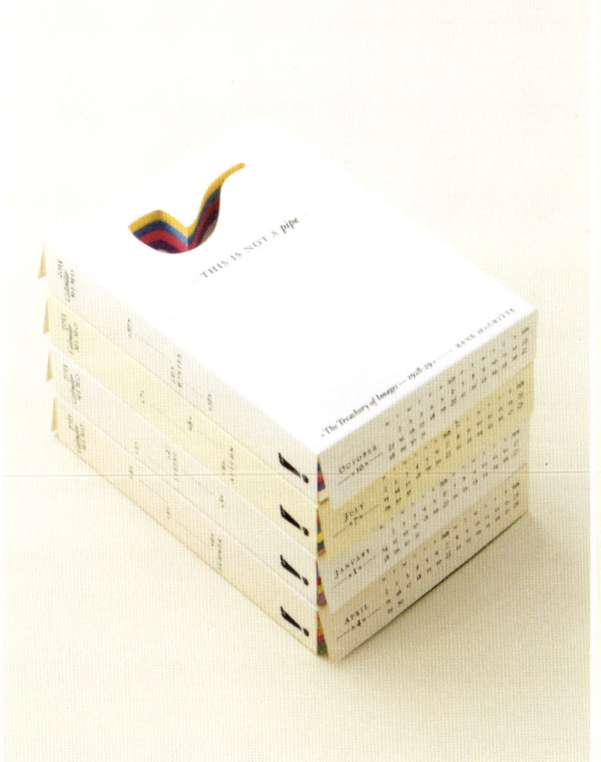
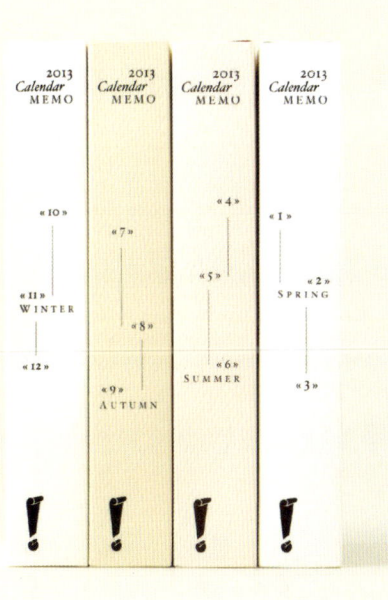

Fedrigoni Calendar 2015

Design — Chris Ong
Photography — Suki Mok
Collaboration — Sarah Temple

Having a simple, yet multi-functional calendar is important to promote Fedrigoni's "Woodstock" paper range. Inspired by book sculptures and folds that are visually intriguing, Chris Ong designed a calendar that could systematically evolve into a mini desk sculpture. Each day is perforated, so the calendar can also double as a sample book. The user has a choice to either fold for the next day, or take away the paper for further use.

Sugar for Everyday

Studio   DMG
Design   Ivan Pivovarov
Copy-writing Aleksandr Kizik

Sugar for Everyday, is a hilarious take on a desktop calendar. Inspired by horses and their love of sugar cubes, this minimal black box is comprised of these miniature blocks that make up the entire calendar year. For those who have a bit of a sweet tooth, it is a great way to have your daily dose of sugar and eat it too.

Calendar was developed for the company "DMG" as a gift for New Year. The idea of the calendar is based on the famous "ritual" appeasement of the horse (symbol for the year), treating it with a piece of sugar.

JUL 30 — International Day of Friendship

Sky Goodies Doodle Monthly Planner

Design   Sky Goodies Products And Applications Private Limited
Photography The Sky Goodies creative team

Organizing your tasks should be fun as well, shouldn't it? Here is a lovely hand-drawn monthly planner to jot down and organize your events, birthdays, reminders or activities. 12 different unique hand-drawn monthly pages, full of whimsical doodles, to add joy to mundane tasks.

This was designed as a printable and also as a set of printed sheets. As a printable the advantage is that it can be printed on a home printer and uses very little ink.

The illustrations of the months are of the following subjects:

1. January: Picture frames on a wall and a cosy arm chair
2. February: A buzzing bee hive
3. March: A field on a farm
4. April: Jars on a shelf
5. May: A wall with a window
6. June: Raindrops and an umbrella
7. July: A grand old tree with a swing and a doggy
8. August: A blimp with two doggies
9. September: Fish find some treasure
10. October: Autumn leaves, waiting to be eaten by a caterpillar
11. November: A shelf at home
12. December: Cupcakes and goodies

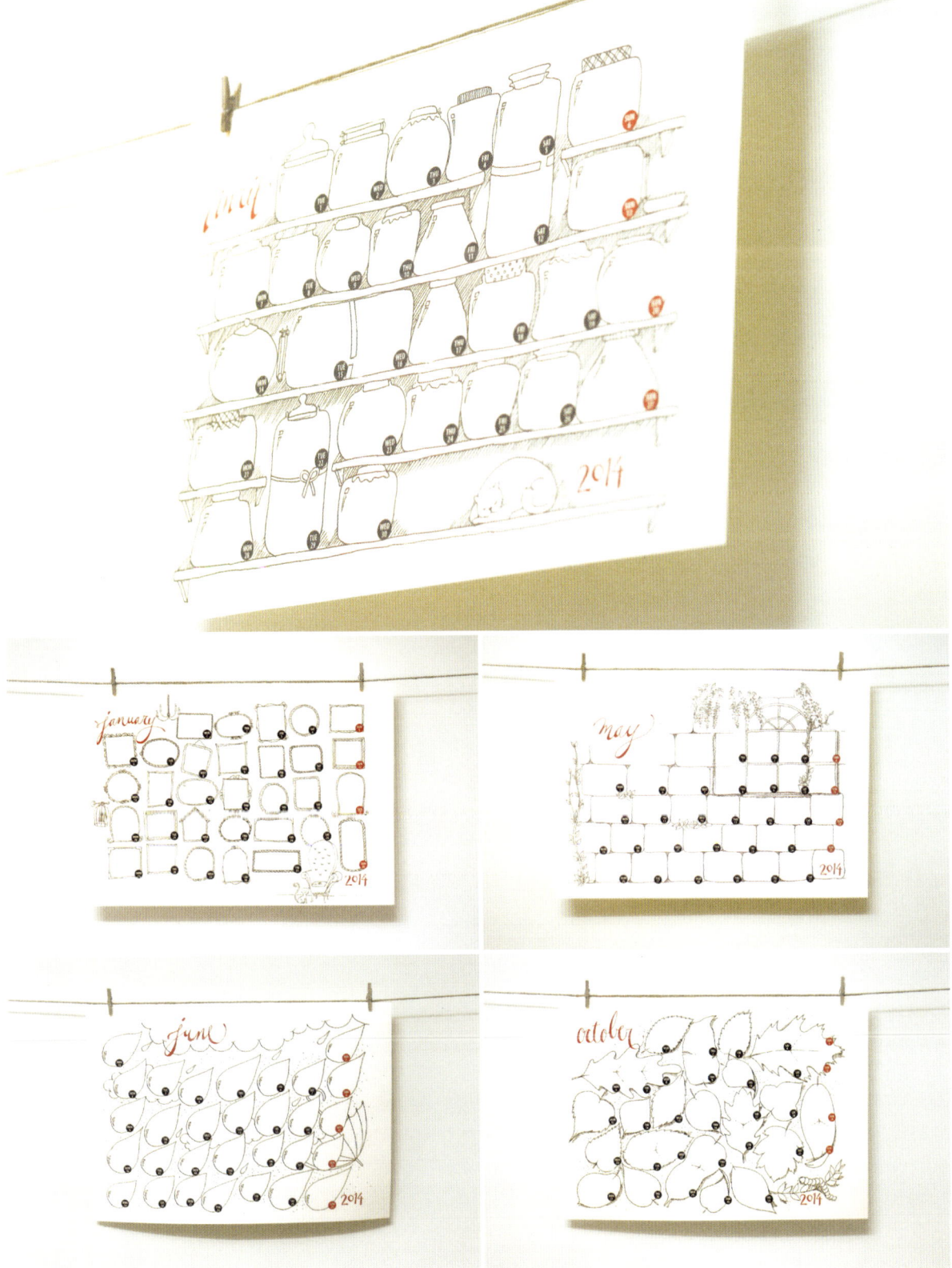

AUG
1

World Scout Scarf Day (International)

IZOLYATSIA 2013

Design Dima Sergeev

The task is to create a creative and easy-to-produce calendar using only recycled materials. It should fit in a A3-sized postal envelope and be lightweight.

Dima Sergeev made a deal with one of the local factories that produces corrugated cardboard to make A3 sheets with little windows for numbers. A3 format laser printer were used to print internal blocks with a calendar grid on kraft paper and tied together with a binder. The binder is used as a fastener and hook at the same time.

Dima Sergeev also produced a stamp used to print the foundation logo on the cover page. The result is an Eco-calendar which is really useful, handy and easy to assemble. These calendars make ideal presents for IZOLYATSIA friends for the New Year holidays. At the moment 200 pieces were sent around the world.

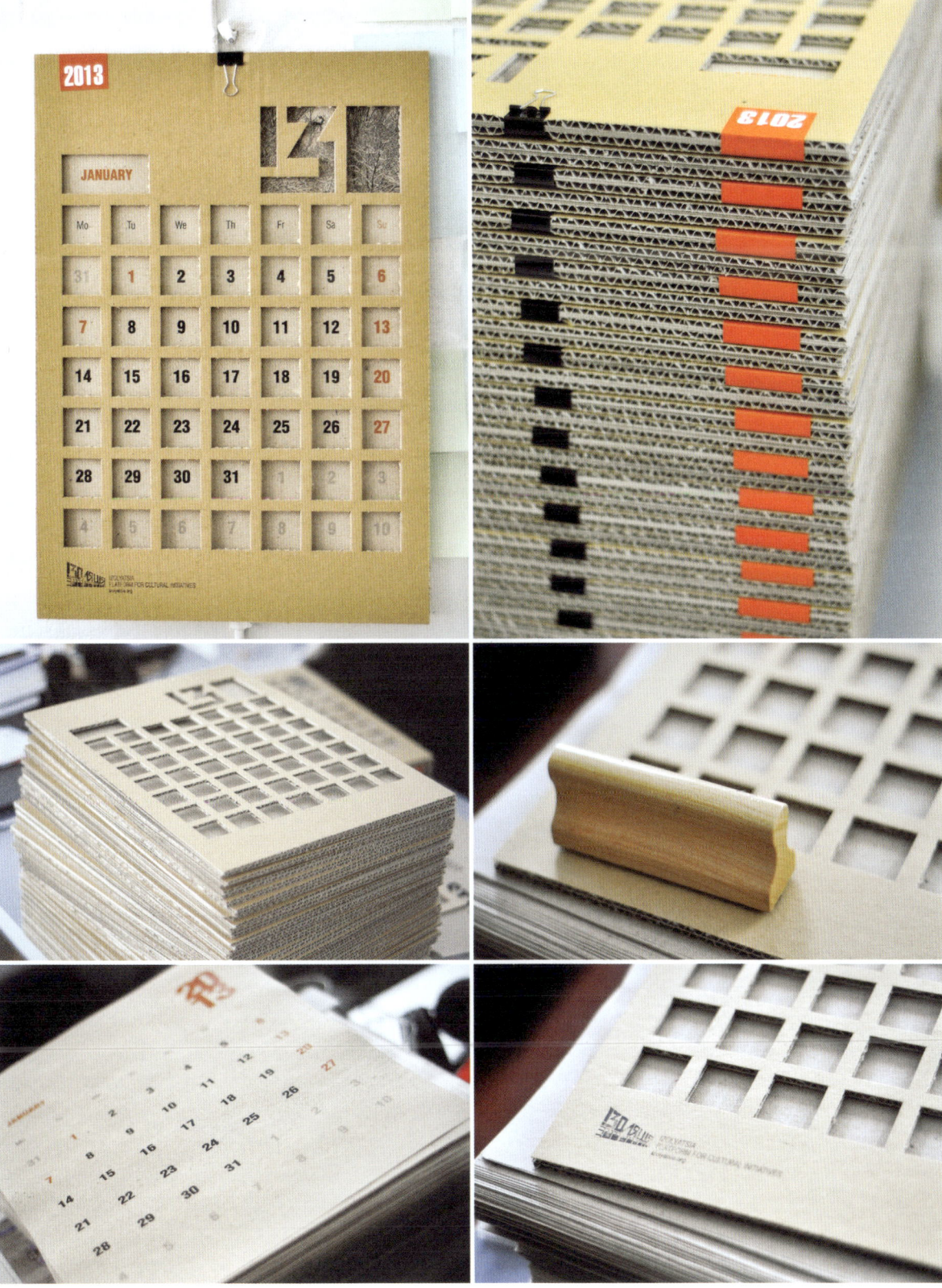

Flag Day (Venezuela)

Fragile Pocket Calendar

Design — Kostantia Manthou
Printing — Legno (Milan, Italy)

AUG 4

Coast Guard Day (U.S.)

Fragile Pocket Calendar is a tiny fold-able and portable calendar, meant only for the important stuff. In a world where digital planners, organizers and diaries are constantly synced with every aspect of life, some events may need to stay in an analogue format as a reminder of an old era or simply as a form of expressing oneself analogically. The main material in use is a lightweight paper, in order to increase the feeling of fragility thus increasing the importance of the calendar and the necessity to protect and cherish it among with its important contents.

AUG 5

Victory and Homeland Thanksgiving Day and the Day of Croatian defenders (Croatia)

Gráficas Unidas Calendar

Studio   Noblanco
Design   Gráficas Unidas
Photography   Diana Montoya,
                  Alfonso Posada
Collaboration   A group of illustrators and
                  designer from Medellin

A calendar is the excuse to reunite 12 illustrators, artists and graphic designers. The final piece will be 12 mini artworks.

AUG
7

Republic Day (Côte d'Ivoire)

Happy 12 Month 2010

Client Rice Garden
Studio Victor Branding Design Corp

Rice Garden's 2010 calendar is designed around the core concept of the brand — passing the taste of happiness. Designed to resemble a recipe book with rice as the main ingredient, each month introduces an authentic cuisine and ancient cooking methods using rice. Besides explaining the benefits of rice, the calendar also provides step-by-step instructions on how to cook these dishes, as well as providing information in Taiwanese culture. These provides added value to the calendar and re-emphasize the core concept of conveying happiness through the fragrance of rice.

AUG 9

International Day of the World's Indigenous People

Tastee Toaster Calendar

Studio Signorina Navarra | Doo Daa Studio
Design Angela Navarra

Being a long time fan of toasters, it was only natural that I would end up making a toaster that could be on display on my office desk. This product was a side project of mine that turned into a reality. From the hand-lettered months of the year, design, paper, and layout, I learned and was inspired throughout every phase.

This paper toy calendar was modelled after a beloved kitchen appliance and a "tastee" breakfast treat. It comes with six hand-lettered toast slices, each featuring two months of the year (front & back). All components are printed on recycled paper, off-set printed with score lines for easy folding.

Calendario Madera

Design Soom Studio

Wopsan Group, a client of Soom Studio's, wanted to create a useful and original gift for their contributors, and not simply a typical piece of merchandising. We therefore decided to create a perpetual calendar made from oak and engraved using laser.

TANGRAM

Client NDI S.A.
Studio TOFU Studio / Poland
Design Iwona Duczmal

A calendar commissioned by a construction company. Aside from the calendar, the kit includes wooden blocks, which can be used to create forms depicted on particular calendar cards. This calendar is awarded a Silver Medal at the International Calendar Contest, VIDICAL 2013.

AUG 13

International Lefthanders Day

AUG 14

Pramuka Day (Indonesia)

Dot to Date

Design — Dan Usiskin
Collaborators — Hidden Art

Calendars are often pretty mundane things. However, Dot to Date is a fun, informal calendar that plays with the rituals and patterns we have in our adult life by contrasting them with the childhood activity of dot-to-dot.

The calender is received in a packaging that converts into a picture frame to display the upcoming monthly creations. The cards are all blank except for the numbered dots that are representative of each day and a little architectural detail. As the days, weeks and months go by, the dots are joined by the user to reveal a London Landmark.

The format provides a framework to be used, customised, coloured and scribbled on. As time goes on it becomes a more emotive, personal and unique object. Taking on the personality of the user, becoming more valuable in the process.

AUG 17

Smile and Wave to Tourists International Day

2014 Isometric Risograph Calendar

Studio Paper Pusher
Design Jp King

This 2014 Calendar explores the illusory depth of isometric shapes through a nostalgic use of half-tone, overprinting spot colours, and fibrous kraft paper. Printed using the dynamic Risograph process, a machine which operates as a hybrid between screen printing and photocopying, each page features the use of fluorescent pink ink, which gives each month a luminescent pop. An inherently retro quality to both the content and form honours the modernist traditions of utopian geometry, offering these shapes up to the imagination as possible architectural models, abstract infographics, or even microbiological specimens.

This artefact pushes against the myth that risograph is a sloppy and inaccurate process. Through careful attention to detail, Paper Pusher has been able to push this machine to near perfection. Printed on a RISO RP 3700 using Blue, Yellow, and Fluro Pink inks, all corners are rounded with a 3/8" radius die, and all twelve pages are bound and hung using a single black bulldog clip.

2014 Beer + Food Pairings Calendar

Studio   Redcruiser
Design   Heidi Schweigert
Photography   Heidi Schweigert

Each month features an illustrated variety of beer and an ideal food mate: Pale Ale and Tomato Soup; Hefeweizen and Bacon/Eggs; IPA and Quesadillas; Lager and Hot Dog; Imperial Stout and Ice Cream; Brown Ale and Sweet Potato Fries. The calendar is displayed with a 1 – 1/4 inch bulldog clip. When finished with the calendar, each month can be trimmed to be used as art or postcards. Printed on 100% post consumer waste paper (FSC certified).

Past & Future Calendar

Studio   BITRI

Past & Future is not a common calendar. It consists of a carefully crafted wooden box with two drawers, one for the future and the other for the past. The future drawer contains a sheet of fine paper for each day that is kept at the past drawer after being used. The present? Well, the present happens when paper is being written on, as it can't be hidden inside a box.

Besides its concept, the secret of this calendar is in its details. Materials are of exceptional quality, from wood to paper and fabric. Everything is manually assembled, an homage to traditional crafts and a way to guarantee a unique product. Let us also not forget that the graphic design is quietly shown through typographic solutions and their printing or engraving methods. This makes Past & Future a collectable piece, one you can renovate each year and build an archive with.

Year in Stitches Calendar Kit

Studio   Heather Lins Home
Design   Heather Lins

The Year in Stitches Calendar is a kit — a contemporary take on the cross stitch sampler. Each month, there is a different typographic design to stitch. It's super-easy! Just poke and stitch. No embroidery or cross stitch skills are required.

AUG 22

Madras Day (Chennai, India)

Stitch the Stars Calendar Kit

Studio   Heather Lins Home
Design   Heather Lins

The Stitch the Stars Calendar is a kit. Each month is screen printed with a glow-in-the-dark constellation. Connect the dots using the glow-in-the-dark embroidery thread and needle provided. It's super-easy! No embroidery skills are required.

AUG 23

European Day of Remembrance for Victims of Stalinism and Nazism

2012 Calendar

Studio   Qube Studio (Singapore)
Art Direction   Quentin Berryman
Design   Quentin Berryman
Typography   Quentin Berryman

For Qube's 2012 calendar, we wanted to combine the everyday with people's love of taking notes, leaving notes, jotting down, scribbling etc. The challenge was how to combine the two and still make it aesthetically pleasing and useful. After some creative soul searching, we developed a TAKE NOTE "block" which combined 365 days with a unique set of notes on the reverse of each day. The box had two sides "Take Note" on one side for the days and "Noted" on the other for the note papers. The national holidays were treated slightly differently using a more exotic stock and printing techniques, including de-bossing and foil stamping. We also included the Chinese calendar dates which was very typographically challenging. The packaging also worked as a stand making the complete package versatile and unique.

AUG
25

Soldier's Day (Brazil)

FAIRYTALES 2015

Studio TOFU Studio / Poland
Art Direction Adam Chylinski,
 Iwona Duczmal
Design Adam Chylinski,
 Iwona Duczmal,
 Zuza Zamorska,
 Mikołaj Sałek;
Management Daniel Naborowski
Photography Paweł Klein, Iza Sawicka
Presentation Adrian Samselski
Printing Drukarnia NORMEX
Sponsors Gdanska Akademia
 Bankowa / European
 Financial Congress,
 TOFU Studio,
 Drukarnia NORMEX.

A non-profit wall calendar made as a gift for the Pomeranian Hospice for Children.

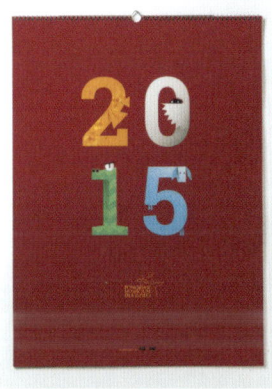

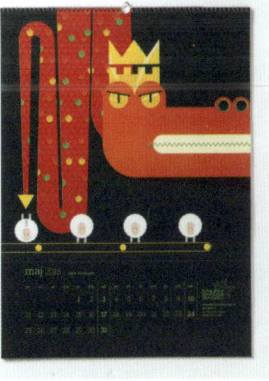
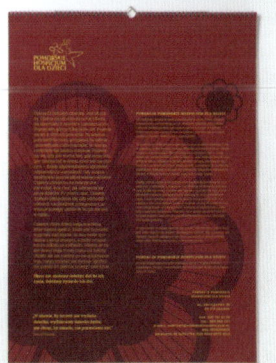

AUG 27 — Lyndon Baines Johnson Day (Texas)

3D Rock Show Calendar

Design — Onion Design Associates
Collaboration — Andrew Wang

The calendar was printed with Neenah double-sided classic column with the 3D glasses die-cut out on to the same sheet of paper. One side is printed metallic black ink on black paper. The inside was printed with two overlapping Pantone red and blue colour for the 3D effect.

AUG
29

International Day against Nuclear Tests

Typographic Calendar

Design   Alexis Bourceret

This is a typographic calendar, where each month is represented by a different typeface. Alexis Bourceret choose to represent the greatest typographic families to show their diversity to the public, and tried to play with each figure to create a symbol that was arranged in the corners of each card to simulate a card game.

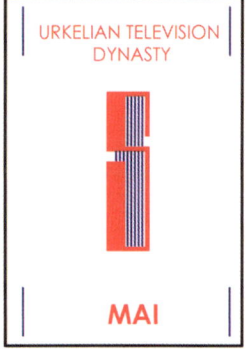  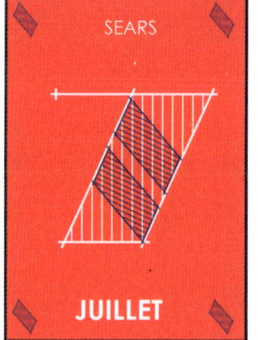 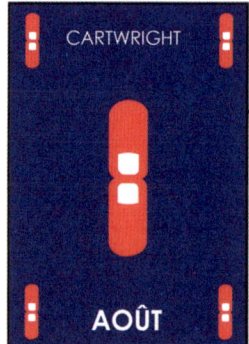
  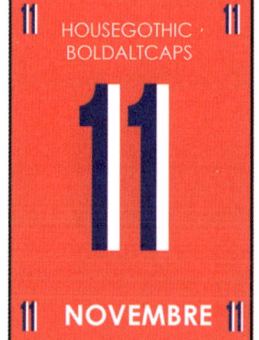 

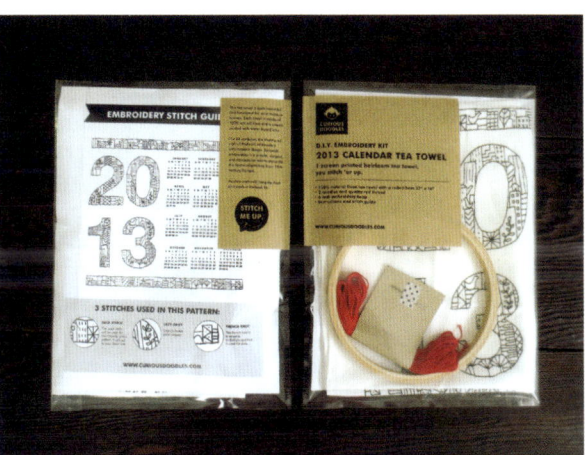

2013 Tea Towel Calendar

Studio CuriousDoodles
Design Laura Trimell

This tea towel is part of a DIY embroidery kit, featuring linen fabric and a screen-printed cityscape pattern. The vibrant red floss is a nod to a traditional embroidery style known as Redwork.

AUG 31

Day of Solidarity and Freedom (Poland)

upstruct calendar 2013

Studio   upstruct
Design   Toni Harzer, Lars Trautmann

Illustrative screen-print calendar 2013. A poster in A1 size with 12 beautiful monthly illustrations and a minimalistic calendar. It is a two colour screen-print (black and neon-orange) on 240 grams Munken Lynx stock and has an edition of 75 copies.

SEP 1 — Journalist Day (Republic of China)

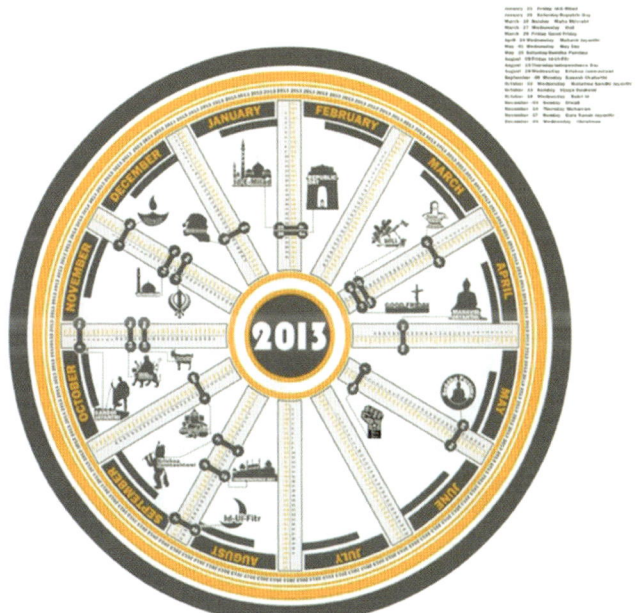

3D Infographic Calender

Design   Mohit Lakhmani

3D Infographic Calendar suggests a 3 dimensional calendar which can not only be seen but can also be touched. This handmade paper crafted art piece is made of 39 A4 sized papers which have been printed first and joined together to give it a grand look of a hanging calendar.

Calendars are an important element in everyone's life — for the businessmen or the common men. This 3d model will not only let you know the dates but also highlights or feature a unique marker for special dates or festive dates, which makes it stand out from the rest.

2012 Vintage Handkerchief Calendar

Studio Mink Letterpress
Design Nicole Lissenden
Photography Nicole Lissenden

Two colour letterpress prints of vintage handkerchiefs in various styles.

Calendar 2014 — 5th Element

Design   Nikita Ivanov

We know that a year consists of twelve months, to each of them, there corresponds a certain sign of a zodiac circle. Each of these signs bears with itself, one of four natural elements and one of four primitive elements:

As we know, the person is a reflection of the boundless Universe, and as a source and the generator of energy. From this judgment, nothing is constant and predetermined. Under what zodiac sign the person wouldn't be born, by what influence of planets wouldn't be influenced, what element in it wouldn't dominate, — each of us is the centre, the fifth element connecting all four.

We are capable to study, to manoeuvre and go deep into an essence of everyone. We are capable to observe, to listen, interacting with each other. We are capable to give, so, we can take. But based on the market, people studied it for the monetary relations, and unfortunately, very few people make progress in the personal relations. The understanding between people often becomes isolated, where the capitalist world absorbs feelings of people so much so that they simply avoid communication.

COLOURFUL: A Letterpress Desk Calendar

Design The Letterpress Shoppe
Photography Mel Louie

Designed by The Letterpress Shoppe, COLOURFUL is a monthly desk calendar that is printed with a 50-year-old vintage platen press. It is printed on 100% cotton, extra thick card stock made from textile scraps, making it a tree-free eco-friendly product. Each month has a unique design, balanced with clean typography in a range of colours. It includes a wooden stand that can be re-used for years to come.

SEP 6

Pregnancy and Infant Loss Remembrance Day (United States)

Life Calendars:
Love Life, Day by Day

Studio   Wap-oh!
Design   Raquel Catalan

Life Calendar: Love Life, Day by Day is a unique and intimate calendar that summarises graphically your life as a couple. A mini diary to complete with that special person that reflects how much time you have dedicated to each other in different aspects of your relationship. In theory, the more red the more love!

Each day is represented with a clear heart that is meant to be completed according to your life as a couple. The heart is divided into four parts: activities, talking, pampering and sex. You can also add small notes that you want to remember.

The calendar is valid for any year. There are 365 hearts in the calendar, one per day, numbered and ordered by month. You can start the first day of the year or in any special date, like for example an anniversary. Once finished, the calendar becomes a very personal keepsake that can decorate a special corner of your home.

SEP 8

International Literacy Day

Calendar ADG

Design Isadora Gonzaga
Photography Isadora Gonzaga

This calendar is created for the institution, ADG Brazil (Graphic Designers Association of Brazil) to be given to the members at the end of the year. The direction for this project was the use of the "sensory design", when the client not only has the original function of the product, but can also has the tactile experience of the calendar.

SEP 10

World Suicide Prevention Day

Gong Xi Fa Cai

Design Calvin Tan, Koay Yee Shin, Tan Say Fin
Photography Calvin Tan, Koay Yee Shin

Malaysia is one of the multi-cultural countries where we celebrate traditional festivals together without the restriction of any races. In Malaysia, we have our own unique way to celebrate our Chinese New Year. This book shares how Malaysians celebrate Chinese New Year. During Chinese New Year, the first thing that comes to your mind is "恭喜發財" (Gong Xi Fa Cai) when you first speak to anyone. It literally means "Congratulations on getting more wealth". Then "紅包拿來" (Hong Bao Na Lai) will be replied humorously. This means "Give me red packet".

The Standard Hotel Calendar

Studio   KK Outlet
Design   KasselsKrammer
Photography Thomas Maileander

The Standard Hotel is always striving for perfection. To help them get better, they listen to the suggestions of their patrons and take them more seriously than most. So serious in fact, that they used them as the inspiration for their 2014 calendar.

Using Weiner dogs in buns and haunted TV screens, the calendar brings to life twelve of the most absurd notes dropped into The Standard's suggestion box.

The result is a collection of photographs that visualize completely rational requests & comments such as, "My girlfriend and I spent lots of money at the bar and on room service. Any compensation would be greatly appreciated." and "I lost my kush. Where's my kush?"

Each month is dedicated to a favourite guest letter, comment or request the hotel received in 2013. They were gratefully received and joyfully re-enacted by The Standard staff.

Whilst having breakfast in the hotel, the production team came a cross one of the other guests settling down to his eggs dressed fully in a white smock and sporting a saviour like beard. He was immediately cast to play Jesus in a re-enactment of the following comment, "Thank you for providing a refuge to recover from the harsh world of Los Angeles and its dog-eat-dog media business… I have been reborn a better man."

Other shots were based on internet pranks, such as filling the hallway with 300 cups of water to accompany, "Hey Standard, thanks a plenty for the most epic hangover of my life. And thanks even more for rehydrating me the next day. Sincerely."

The concept was devised by communications agency, KasselsKrammer in collaboration with The Standard and shot by French photographer Thomas Maileander on location in the hotels.

Produced in a high gloss vibrant red the calendar brings a bit of The Standard glamour and fun to every wall it adorns. Bring on 2014!

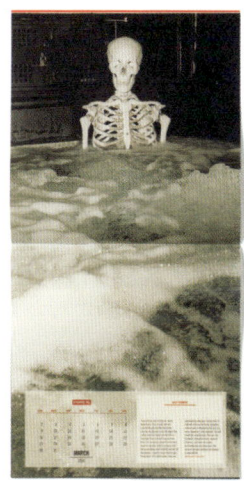

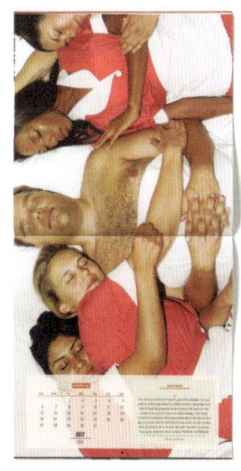

SEP 14

Hindi Day (India)

2013 A Dozen Eggs Calendar

Studio — Mink Letterpress
Design — Nicole Lissenden
Photography — Nicole Lissenden

12 letterpress prints of wild bird eggs, of various types and colours.

International Day for the Preservation of the Ozone Layer

WYCINANKA (Paper-Cut)

Studio TOFU Studio / Poland
Design Iwona Duczmal

A calendar commissioned by a financial institution. This calendar is awarded the Grand Prix and the Audience Award at the International Calendar Contest, VIDICAL 2012.

SEP 17

Heroes' Day (Angola)

SEP 19

International Talk Like a Pirate Day

SEP 20

Universal Children's Day (Germany)

Perforated Calendar 2014

Design Snaefrid & Hildigunnur
Photography Vigfus Birgisson

The purpose of this project is to stretch one's understanding and measurement of time. The work itself becomes a part of daily life and is shaped by it. The year gradually erodes until nothing is left as each day is perforated, to be torn off at the end of the day.

2014 Wood Veneer Calendar

Studio   CuriousDoodles
Design   Laura Trimell
Laser Cutting   Darrell Rossman

This calendar is laser cut out of red oak veneer. The design is inspired by the intricate network of veins found in leaves.

The World's Most Eco-Friendly Calendar

Design Sascha Kuntze, Jesse Bray, Irfan Ghani, Conrad Theron

The answer to a century old brief. With millions of calendars produced every year, and everyone switching to digital calendars, we didn't see a need to create yet another typical calendar that would end up in the bin. So we created the world's most eco-friendly calendar made of 99.9% recycled materials and entirely carbon-offset. It comes without extra packaging and lasts for years.

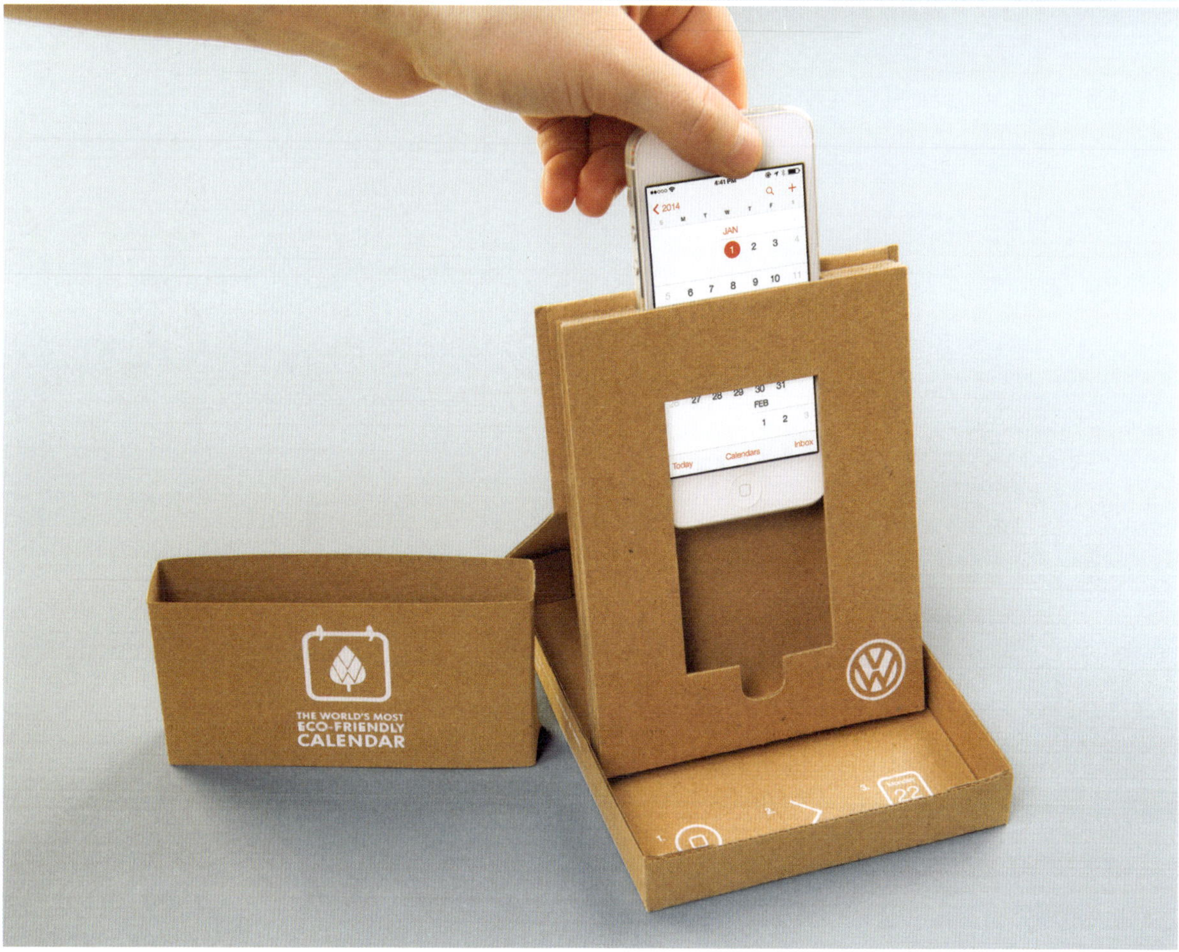

SEP
24

National Punctuation Day (United States)

Chocolates With Attitude 2011

Studio   Bessermachen Designstudio

For the third year in a row, Brandhouse and Bessermachen Designstudio has created a box of chocolates that are to die for. One big and beautiful box contains 12 smaller boxes and each box represents an archetype/personality in a typographic solution. The personality is expressed through a unique quote, a unique design and a unique type of chocolate. The design differentiates the 12 personalities with a diverse and colourful use of typography and the small boxes are round, like tiny hat boxes. The chocolate is created by Coca Luxury Chocolates from unique recipes. Everything was developed from the ground amd the chocolate's taste were selected to fit each personality. Life is like a box of chocolates.

SEP
27

World Tourism Day

SEP 28 — World Rabies Day

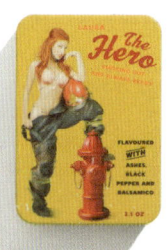

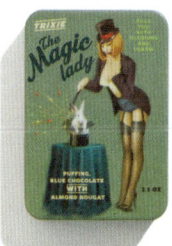

SEP
30

Blasphemy Day

YCN Fedrigoni 2015 Desk Calendar

Design   Laura Wallbridge-Bruce
Photography   Laura Wallbridge-Bruce
Collaboration   YCN, Fedrigoni

The calendar has been designed for the use of graphic designers and was submitted to the YCN Student Awards. It has been designed in a concertina format, minimising the amount of space taken up on a desk. The shape, taken from the Fedrigoni logo, has been used to create a window, illustrating each of the colours within the "Woodstock" range. The functionality of the calendar is simple and easy. Each month, a different piece of paper is removed and revealed to the recipient. With the different weights listed and the chosen stock highlighted, this also acts as a stock guide for the paper.

As there are 22 colours within the range, each month has two different stock choices displayed together, with December and January being the only two months with just one stock used. This leaves room for potential text such as "Happy New Year" and "Happy Holidays".

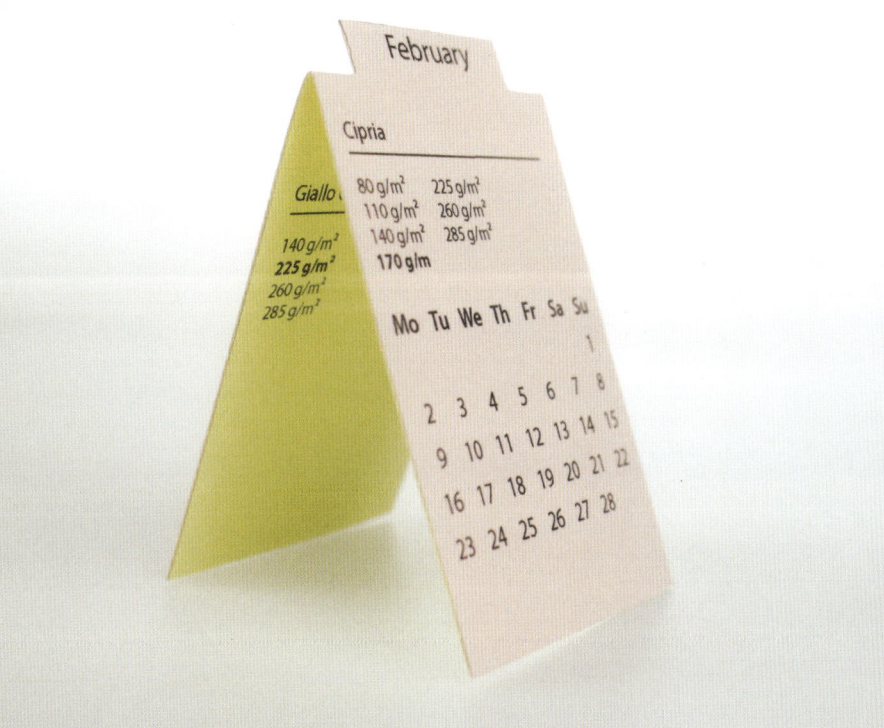

Systemform
Kalender 2014

Design   Alexander Schierl, Anje Jager

A form a day, keeps the chaos away! As making forms is what the Bavarian printer plant Systemform does best, their calendar for 2014 provides clients and partner with a form to fill out for every single day of the year. Starting with New Year's resolutions, the calendar helps you to decide what to eat, what to do and even what not. Weekly statistics track your life and your daily performance will be rated. After 365 days, you might be tired of forms, or instead really getting into them, just like Systemform has been for the last 60 years.

OCT 4 — World Animal Day

Square the Circle

Design   Amelia Krysztofiak

Amelia Krysztofiak created this calendar, playing with geometrical shapes, basic patterns and colours. The inspiration was from Vassily Kandinsky's statement that you can recreate all the numbers using a grid of a circle in a square.

The challenge for this typographic experiment was to keep everything as simple and harmonic as possible. Each month is represented by a combination of planes that creates shapes of the Arabic numbers. Amelia Krysztofiak uses 3 different patterns (dots, stripes & plain) and 3 colours (black, white & pink) in different combinations. As a result, 14 different styles are created to work on dynamic representation of time passing by.

OCT
6

German-American Day (United States)

OCT
8

Navy Day (Peru)

282

Game Calendar 2014

Design Oksana Kapranova

12 board games, each one for each month. Each game is a module, which is built as a cube. There are twister for fingers, darts, soccer, checkers and others. All cubes are collected into tube and this tube hangs on the wall. Every month you take one of the cubes from the bottom and other falls down.

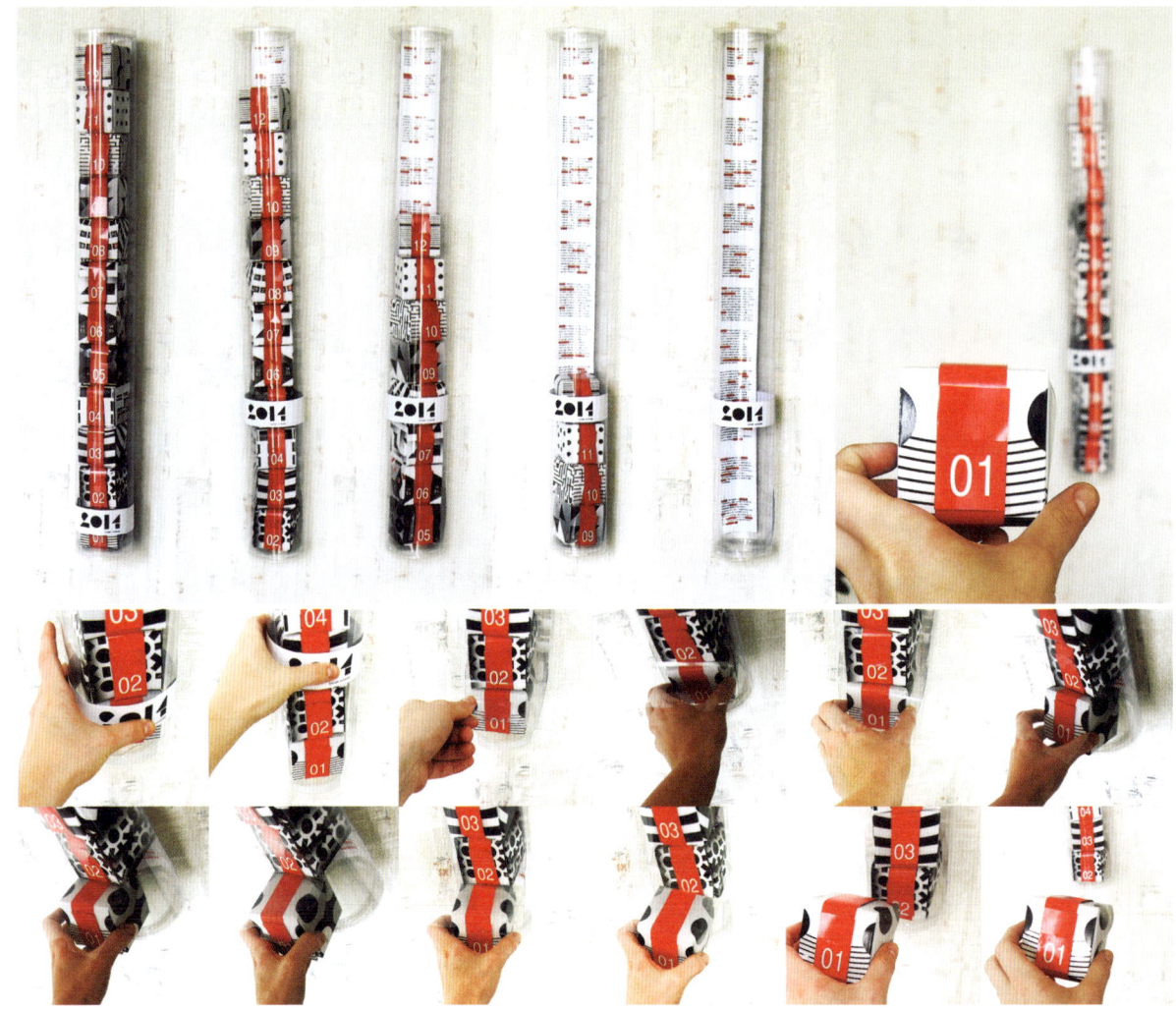

OCT 10 — World Mental Health Day

RuArts Gallery Desk Calendar

Design   Marina Pavlova

RuArts is the Gallery of Modern Art in Moscow. On 7 December, RuArts celebrated seven years since it was founded. A calendar was created for this 7th anniversary, with the idea based on the transformation of the figures. It starts from 7 January 2011 and ends in 8 December 2012 when RuArts turns 8 years old.

OCT
12

Freethought Day (United States)

DAYZ Weekly Planner

Studio LESS THINGZ
Design Magdalena Thur, Michael Augsten

When life is getting faster, it can't hurt to take a step back from the day to day and to take a more measured look at the big picture.

DAYZ weekly planner was conceived as a life design tool. The accordion-folded calendar offers a bird's eye view on life and keeps things in sight. Together with the matching notebook NOTEZ it brings playful creativity back into organizing and creating.

The handmade products are composed of sustainable premium materials: natural rubber, thick cardboard coloured in the pulp, and luxury high volume paper with matte finish.

The planner DAYZ offers three unique ways to look at your time: Hang it on the wall, place it on the table, or take it with you.

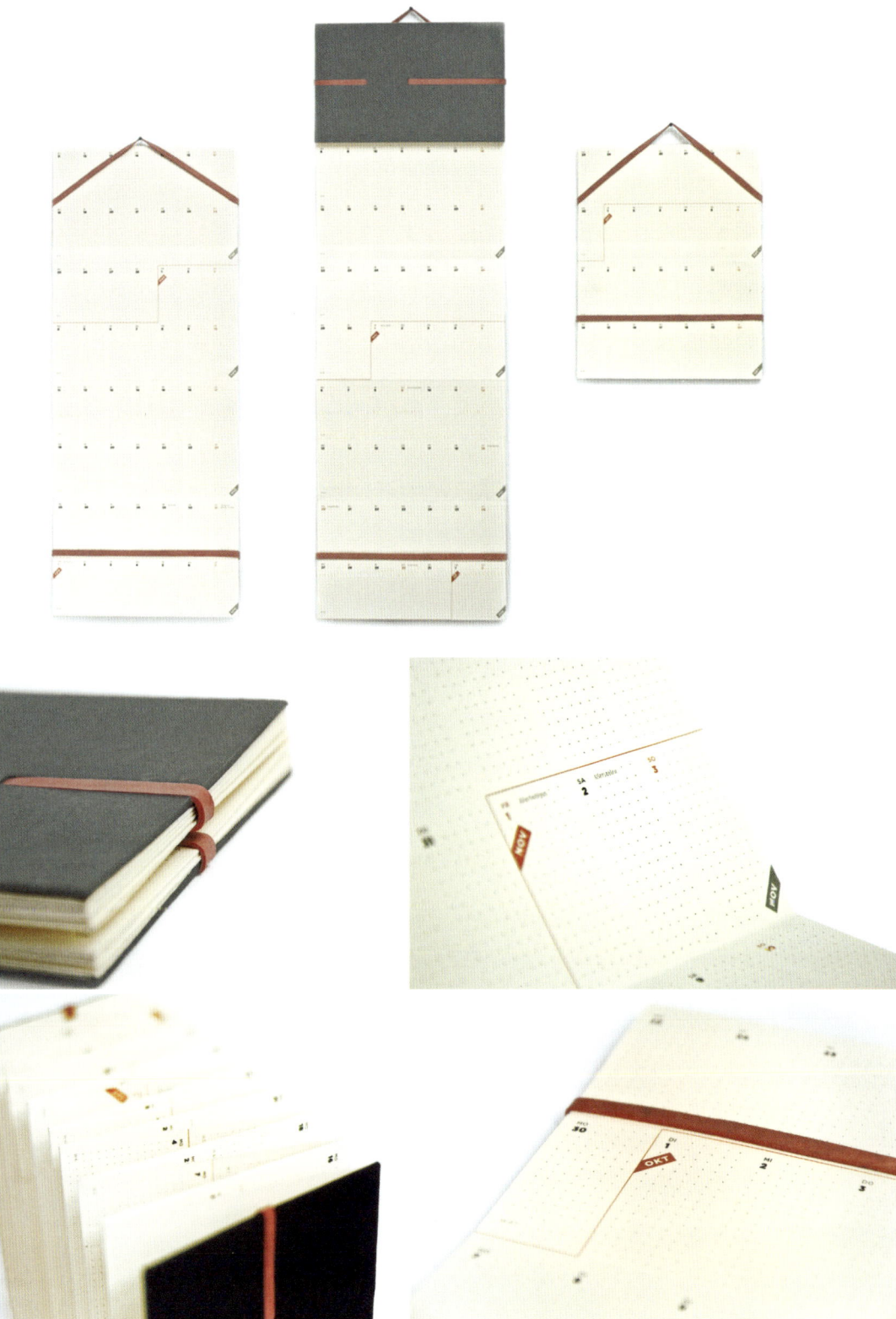

OCT
14

World Standards Day

Fedrigoni Calendar 2015

Design Alan Danby
Photography Alan Danby

This project was part of the YCN student awards competition this year. The brief was to create a desktop calendar for the Fedrigoni Paper Company, which was simple and easy to use, but was also small and useful for desk and office use. Another need was sell their most recent paper product, which was the "Woodstock" range.

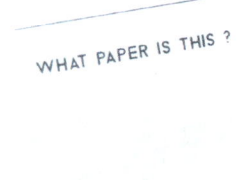

OCT 16 — World Food Day

urbnCal 2013 NORDIC

Design　　　　jollygoodfellow
Photography　　Lisa Tanttu, Esa Tanttu

After requests from Save the Children Sweden and the Taiwanese Bookstore Eslite, jollygoodfellow decided to make a calendar for 2013. This time they picked nice parts from the earlier versions and combined it with some new pictures in Oslo and Reykjavik, to create urbnCal NORDIC.

OCT 17

International Day for the Eradication of Poverty

OCT 18

World Vasectomy Day

OCT
19

Mother Teresa Day (Albania)

Pantone Queen

Studio Leo Burnett
Art Direction Will Thacker, Blake Waters
Copy-writing Will Thacker, Blake Waters
Artwork Prodigious
Creative Imaging Prodigious
Colour Management Prodigious
Photography Andy Rudak

In celebration of Queen Elizabeth II's 60 colourful years on the British Throne, Pantone, the global authority on colour and provider of professional colour standards for the design industries, and leading ad agency, Leo Burnett, have teamed up to launch a limited edition colour guide to mark the Queen's fashion-forward colour statements. For other 60 years, Her Majesty has opted for a full spectrum of perfectly colour co-ordinated ensembles, from the Primrose Yellow she wore at Will and Kate's wedding to the tasteful Lilac Snow outfit she wore to a visit to Northumberland. To mark the Queen's Diamond Jubilee, this bespoke, limited-edition, numbered colour guide is designed to capture and commemorate some of the Queen's most memorable colour choices since her coronation — featuring PANTONE Colour references and citing the date and location that determined her outfit colour choice.

OCT 20

World Statistics Day

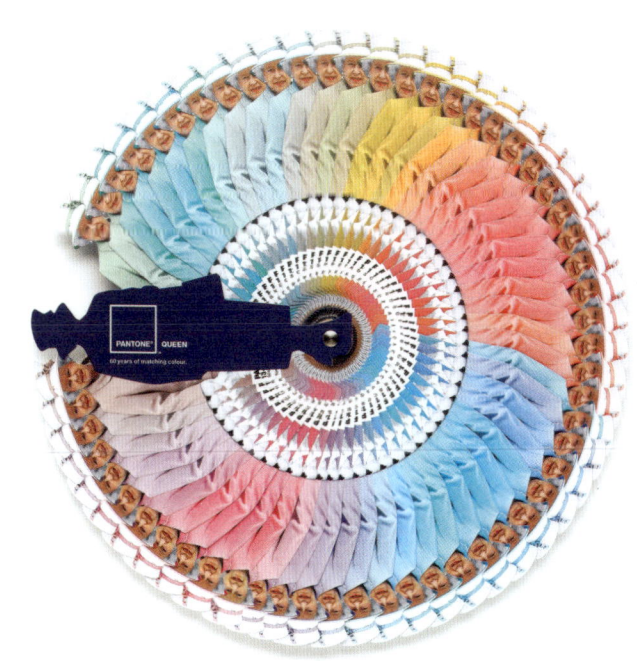

XTRA Calendar 2013

Studio &Larry
Design Larry Peh, Lee Weicong

We were commissioned by XTRA to inaugurate their designer calendar series. The concept is simple: we wanted a calendar that is well-designed and useful. This was in response to typical designer calendars which often sacrificed function for form.

The title, "Designed for every Tom, Dick &Larry", is a pun on a common saying that draws a humorous link to the studio's name while emphasising the calendar's functionality for anyone and everyone. Despite the minimalist approach, the calendar provides a considerable amount of useful information: public holidays, school holidays, term breaks and even Chinese lunar dates. As a subtle reminder, the title block is printed on the reverse side, giving a hint of our design mission through the pages. The calendar can be hung on the wall or used as a desk calendar, depending on individual preferences.

OCT 22

International Stuttering Awareness Day

2014 CALENDAR

Design　　Pixelbox Estudio Gráfico S.L.U.

"A cabin in the woods, a desert island, a balloon trip, by train, by submarine... a Delorean, a castaway, an old lighthouse, a mermaid, a volcano, a murderer... Are you ready? The longest trip of the year begins?"

The idea that time and space are two concepts inseparably related made me see the calendar as a journey, as a journey through a year of 365 days... as a map in which past, present and future are mixed.

Periodic Table of Time

Studio   HAMPER studio, Laboratorium
Design   Ivana Vucic,
              Tomislav Jurica Kacunic
Photography Ivana Vucic,
              Tomislav Jurica Kacunic

This three-part calendar, designed following Mendeleev's strict principles, will help you organize your life, as well as your future. An ideal planner for hard science lovers and world travellers. Originally, PTT calendar was designed as a Christmas gift for Laboratorium studio clients and friends. Scientific, and a "laboratory" look was used to emphasize the experimental nature of studio Laboratorium.

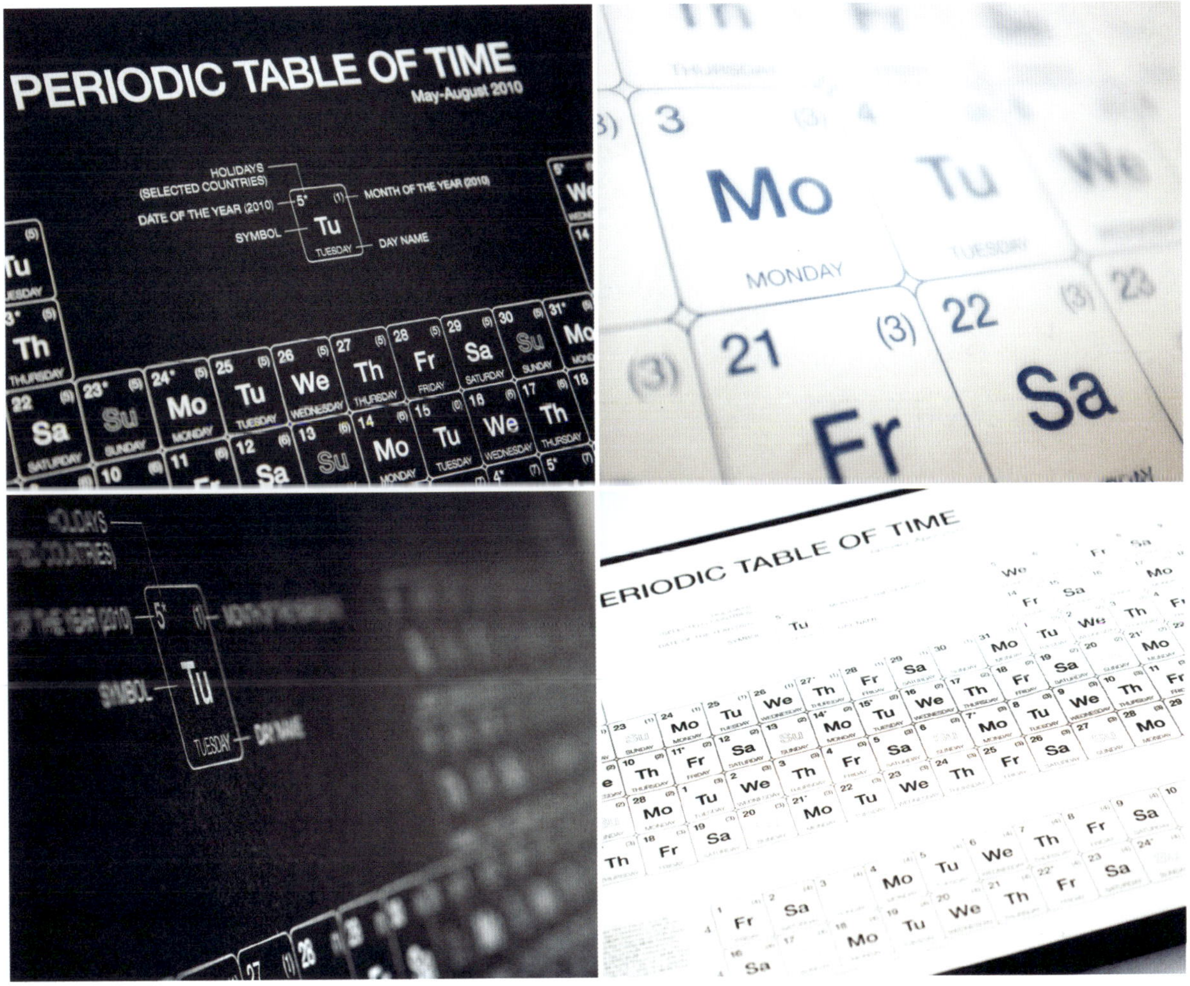

OCT 24

United Nations Day

One Year, One Texture

Design manolab
Photography manolab

Bilingual (in Italian and English), "One year, one texture" is a calendar of the mood. At the beginning the year, the mood is white and full of expectations. Day by day it gets full of experiences, encounters and dreams, and it gets filled up with colours. Towards the end of the year, it is time to take stock. Memory goes back to all the moments spent, and keeps them in a texture full of meanings.

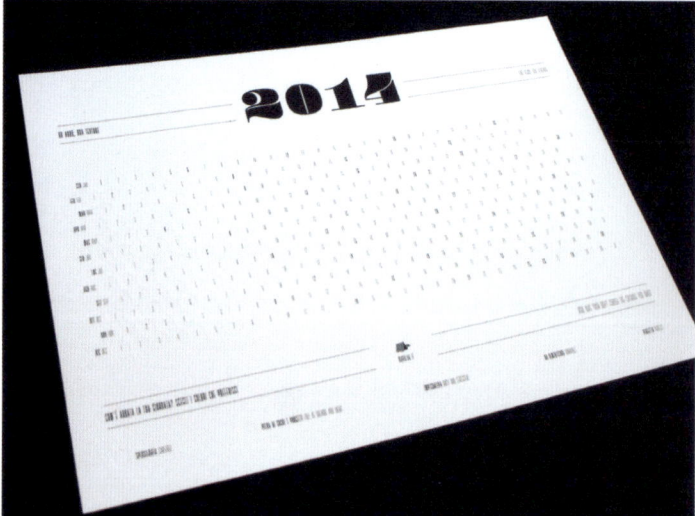

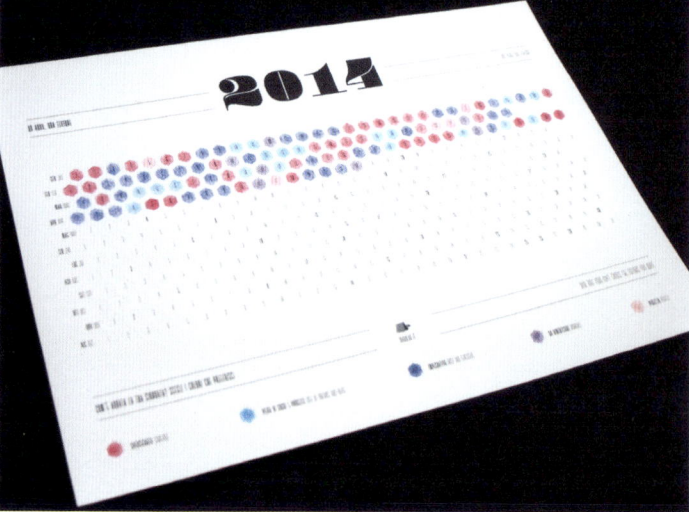

OCT
26

Armed Forces Day (Benin)

2013 Friends Calendar

Design   Azul Piñeiro, Carlos Higuera

It is said that one of the secrets to achieve longevity is based on friendship. Some would like to have a million friends to sing louder, others believe they are luminescent and glow in the dark, some believe soul-mates are real friends, but in actual truth we all have friends. Many would like to appear on a calendar, so we decided to choose 13 of our best friends that might resemble yours, to accompany you throughout 2013 and many more years!

(fig1. Cómo usar tu calendario.)

13

amigo / friend / ami / Freund / ván
صديق / 好друг / 朋友 / רבח
друг / amico / φίλος / ともだち

Dicen que uno de los secretos para alcanzar la longevidad se basa en la amistad. Hay quienes quisieran tener un millón de amigos para cantar más fuerte, otros creen que son luminiscentes y que brillan en la oscuridad o que el hermano del alma es realmente el amigo... lo cierto es que todos tenemos amigos. Muchos quisieran salir en un calendario, por eso decidimos elegir a 13 de nuestros mejores amigos que puede que se parezcan a los tuyos, para que te acompañen durante el 2013 y muchos años más!

	Dom	Lun	Mar	Mie	Jue	Vie	Sab
			01	02	03	04	05
	06	07	08	09	10	11	12
	13	14	15	16	17	18	19
	20	21	22	23	24	25	26
	27	28	29	30	31		

ENE

	Dom	Lun	Mar	Mie	Jue	Vie	Sab
						01	02
	03	04	05	06	07	08	09
	10	11	12	13	14	15	16
	17	18	19	20	21	22	23
	24	25	26	27	28		

FEB

	Dom	Lun	Mar	Mie	Jue	Vie	Sab
					01	02	03
	04	05	06	07	08	09	10
	11	12	13	14	15	16	17
	18	19	20	21	22	23	24
	25	26	27	28	29	30	31

AGO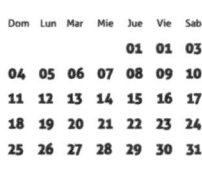

	Dom	Lun	Mar	Mie	Jue	Vie	Sab
		01	02	03	04	05	06
	07	08	09	10	11	12	13
	14	15	16	17	18	19	20
	21	22	23	24	25	26	27
	28	29	30	31			

JUL

	Dom	Lun	Mar	Mie	Jue	Vie	Sab
							01
	02	03	04	05	06	07	08
	09	10	11	12	13	14	15
	16	17	18	19	20	21	22
	23/30	24	25	26	27	28	29

JUN

	Dom	Lun	Mar	Mie	Jue	Vie	Sab
						01	02
	03	04	05	06	07	08	09
	10	11	12	13	14	15	16
	17	18	19	20	21	22	23
	24/31	25	26	27	28	29	30

MAR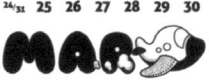

	Dom	Lun	Mar	Mie	Jue	Vie	Sab
		01	02	03	04	05	06
	07	08	09	10	11	12	13
	14	15	16	17	18	19	20
	21	22	23	24	25	26	27
	28	29	30				

ABR

	Dom	Lun	Mar	Mie	Jue	Vie	Sab
				01	02	03	04
	05	06	07	08	09	10	11
	12	13	14	15	16	17	18
	19	20	21	22	23	24	25
	26	27	28	29	30	31	

MAY

OCT **30**

Mischief Night (United States)

The Scent of Time

Studio — Kolle Rebbe GmbH
ECD — Sascha Hanke
Creative Direction — Markus Hammer
Art Direction — Jakob Schumacher, Dennis Schlüter
Copy-writing — Max Wort
Graphic Design — Anja Tränkle
Production — Martin Lühe
Design — Markus Hammer, Jakob Schumacher, Dennis Schlüter
Photography — Dirk Weyer Photography

For 25 years, Kim Weisswange has been creating individual perfumes for royalty, pop stars and Hollywood celebrities. For her 25th anniversary, she sought an idea to thank her loyal customers.

THE SCENT OF TIME is the first calendar that expresses time in the sensual language of perfume. The year, month and day determine the base, heart and head notes. 365 individual fragrances are blended directly onto the skin.

As a result, Weisswange's clientele were delighted. Many of them use THE SCENT OF TIME as an inspiration for their individual orders. The idea was featured in relevant blogs, generating valuable PR.

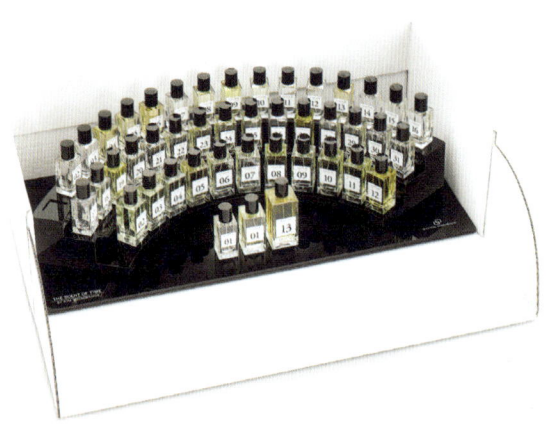

NOV
1

World Vegan Day

Calendar of
Astronomical Events 2014

Design   Margarita Kurtser

This calendar was made for people who are interested in space. I thought that it can be very useful for them to know exactly when the most interesting astronomical events will happen. There are basic calendar elements with marked weekends, lunar calendar and separated months with special days when you can see a certain planet, comet or star. I was impressed with the shape of the galaxy and that is why my calendars are spiral. For comfortable usage, you can cross out past dates and create another spiral line on your calendar.

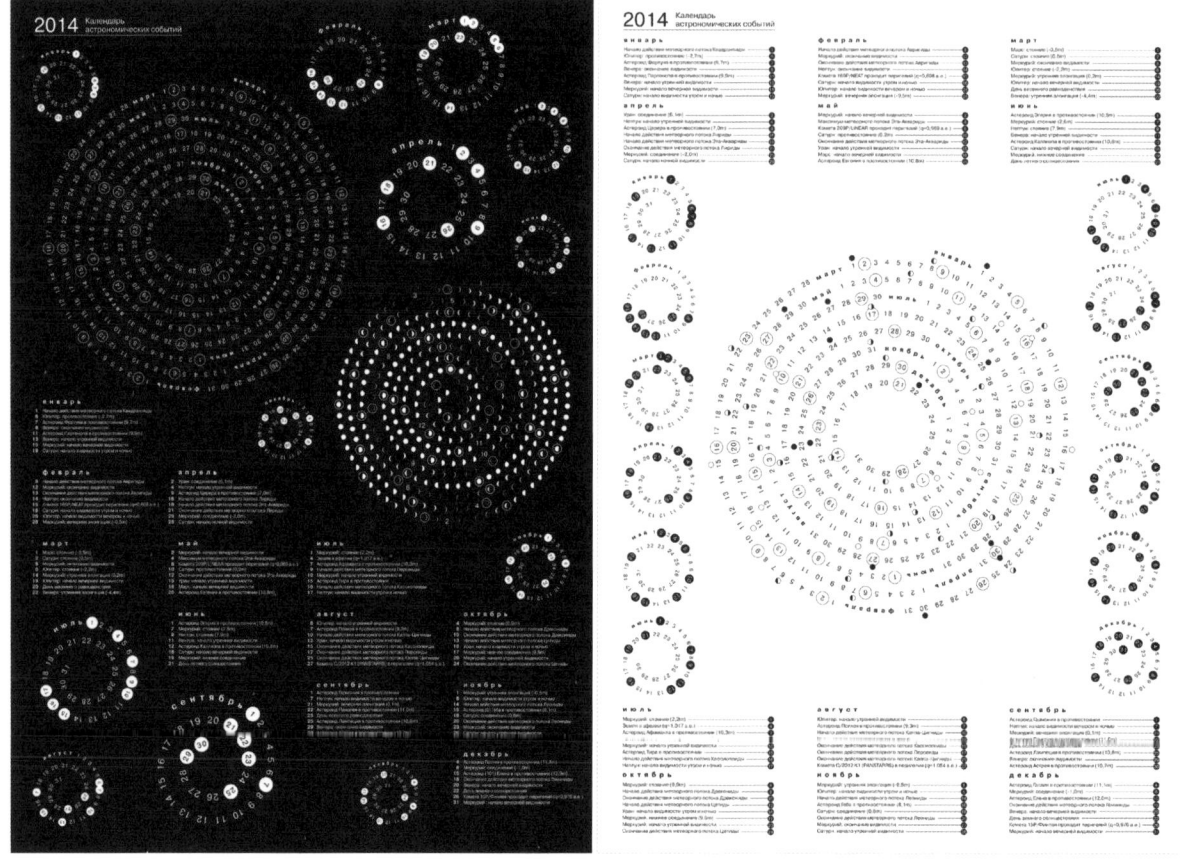

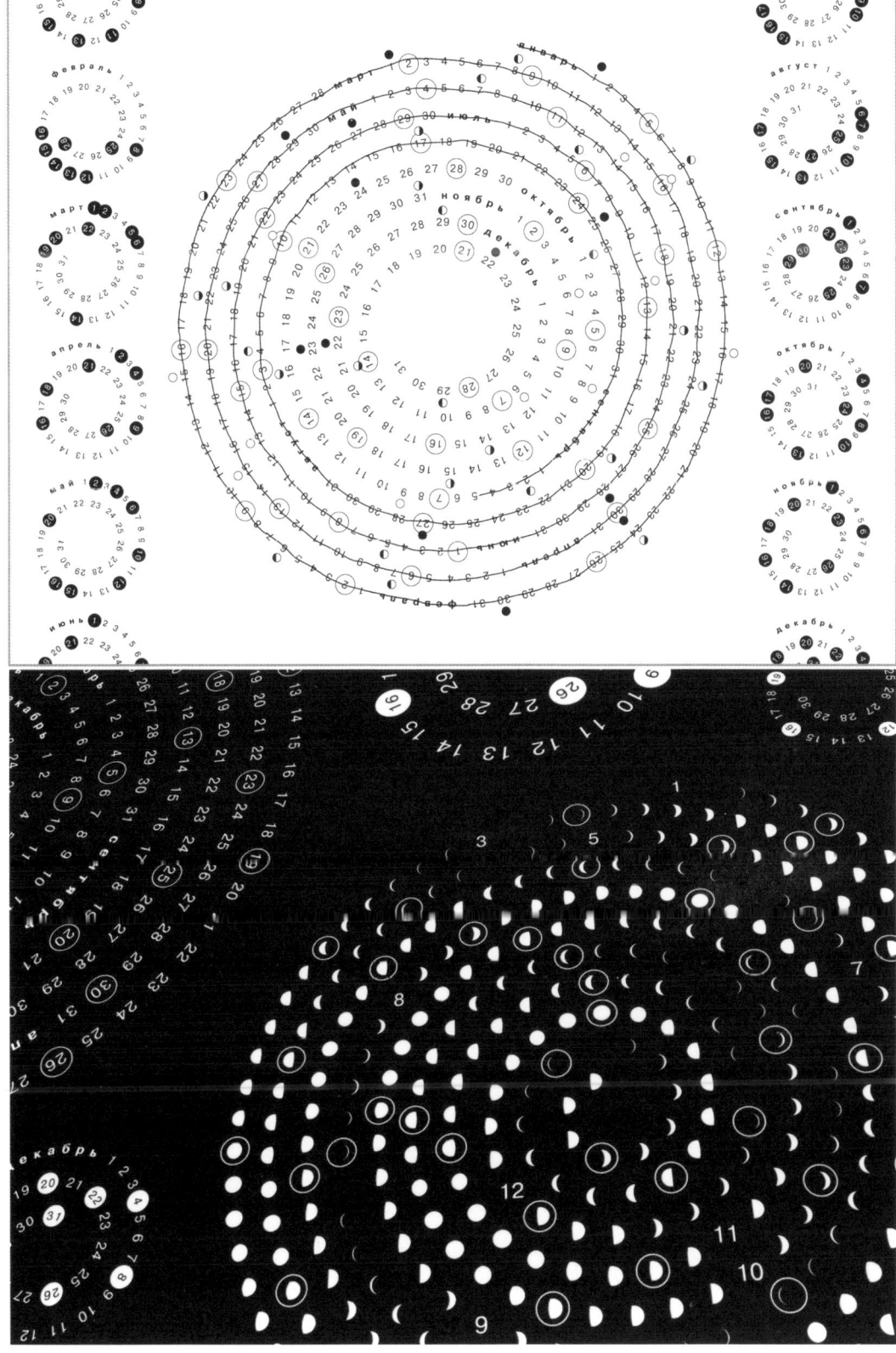

The Brain — 2013 Novelty Calendar

Design Ridhwaan Moolla
Photography Ridhwaan Moolla

The Brain Calendar is a self-initiated conceptual calendar design constructed utilising only basic design elements and principles. The aim with the calendar was to convey the function of primary parts of the brain through the use of typography, illusion and puzzles.

Each month represents a core part of the brain. Some are simply visual representations in the form of an illusion whilst others are puzzles requiring input by the user through the use of a white pen. As such, certain months shown in the images are incomplete. The cover serves as a reference map for the user to discover where these parts are located on a real brain. The calendar, due to its nature is intended for medical or creative working professionals to serve as a show piece in an office space.

Also included with the calendar is a desk hexa-flexagon calendar. It serves as a brain teaser as the user is required to flip and fold the calendar each month in order to eventually fold out all the twelve months of the year.

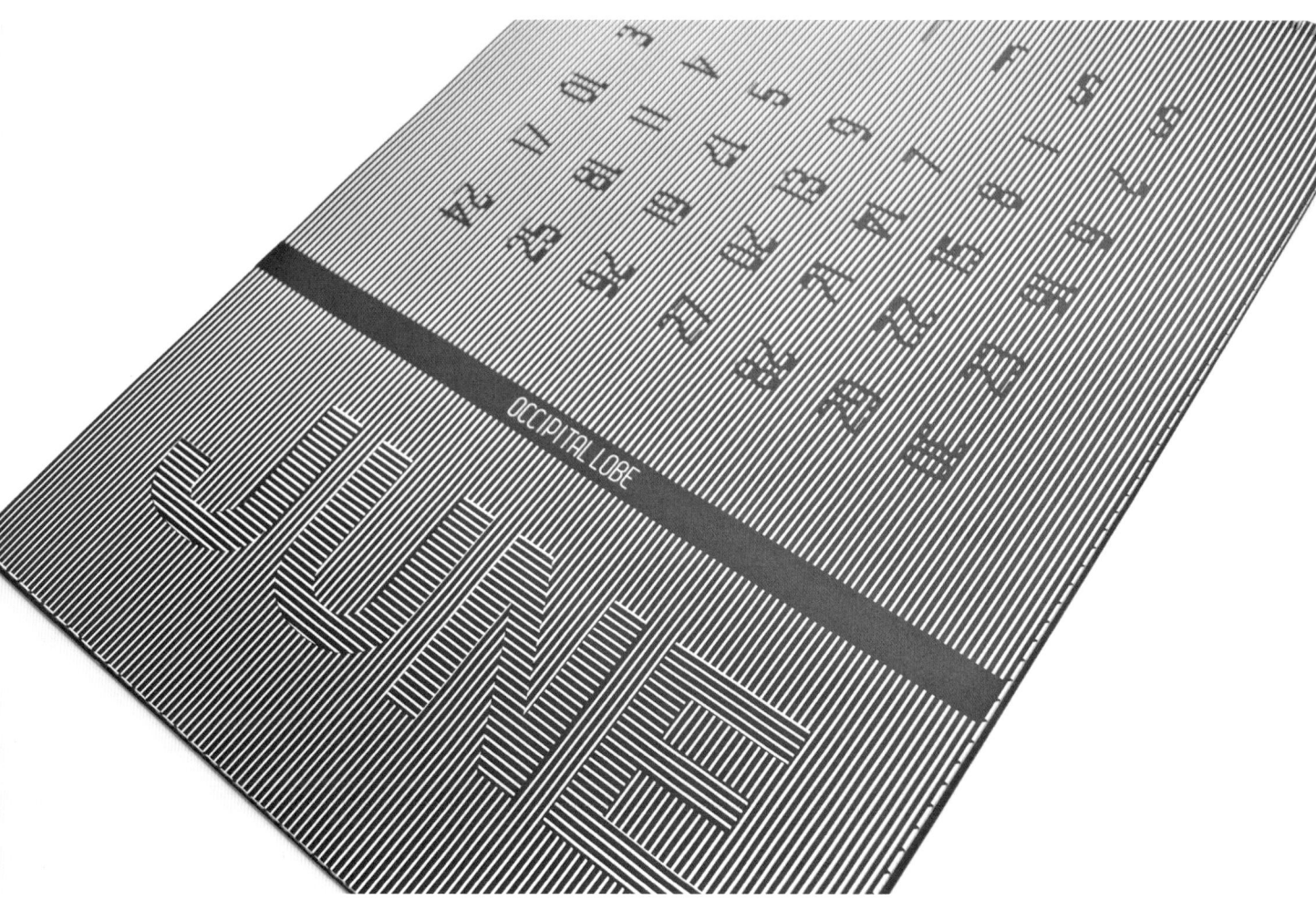

NOV 5

Bonfire Night (Guy Fawkes Night)

Dia Calendar

Design GONÇALO CAMPOS

Called Dia (the Portuguese word for day), with reference to it's one-piece-a-day system that allows you to complete the puzzle as the year goes by. This concept allows you to see the year pass more naturally, letting you interpret the time that passes in a more intuitive and direct way, as well as giving you a notion of how much time have passed and how much time you have left in the month or year.

Because this system is based on modified puzzle pieces that can link to any neighbouring piece, it allows an easy colour-based organization and that turns this time-keeping object into a game of drawing as if each piece was a pixel. This allows an expression of how you see the year, how you personally relate to it, or how you wish it will be.

Each one of the 366 (366 due to leap years) pieces is marked with the day and month that it represents. Because of the flexibility of organising, the calendar is perpetual, and can be adaptable to any year.

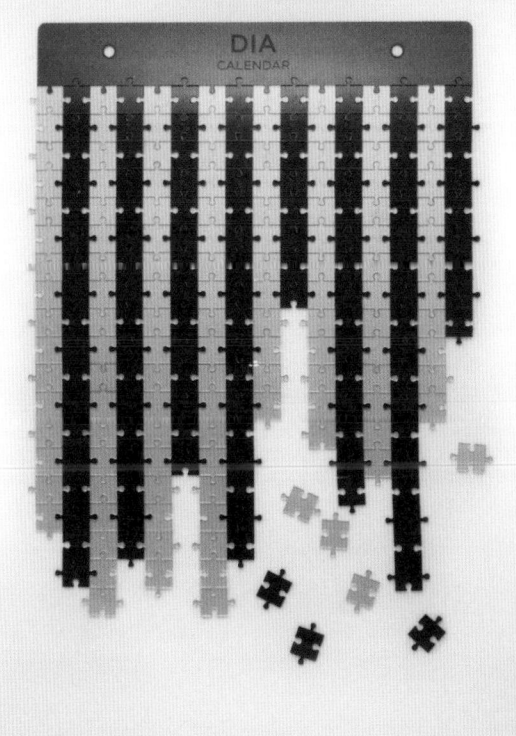

National Revolution and Solidarity Day (Bangladesh)

The Tea Calendar

Studio — Kolle Rebbe GmbH
ECD — Sascha Hanke
Creative Direction — Heiko Schmidt, Kay Eichner
Art Direction — Patrick Schröder
Copy-writing — Julia Meissner
Art Buying — Karen Blome
Production — Martin Lühe, Inch Design Service
Account Management — Kira Middendorf

The Hälssen & Lyon tea calendar is the world's first calendar to feature days made from tea leaves. Exquisitely flavoured and pressed until wafer thin, the 365 calendar days can be individually detached and steeped in hot water — an exceptional combination of the world's oldest advertising medium and the world's oldest beverage. Those who received the tea calendar have the chance — every day this year — to taste the authentic and creative tea products developed by Hälssen & Lyon. This proves that a good calendar can impress the eyes as well as the taste buds.

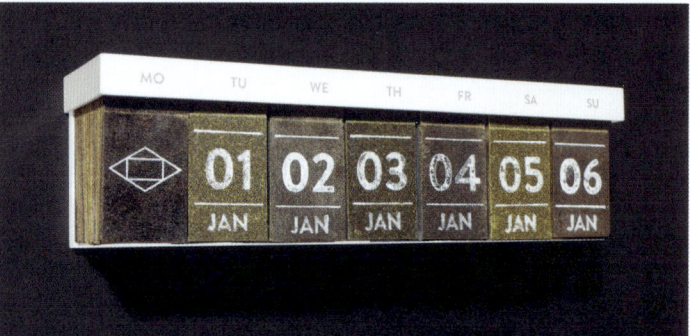
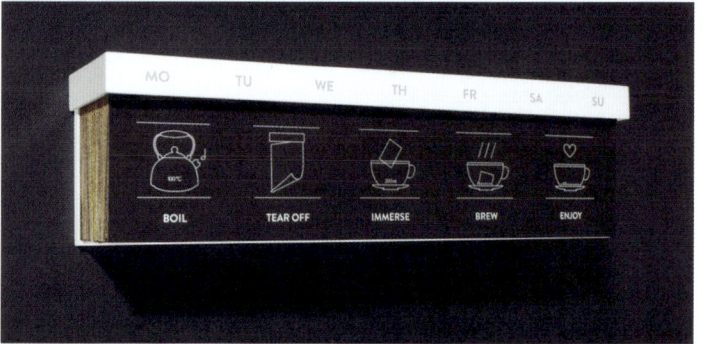

Phenomenal Calendar

Studio Phenomena
Design Akram Dohjoka
Photography Farras Oran

The idea of the calendar was inspired from the clothes rack with a customized die cut for each season, under the line "You're covered!!".

NOV
11

Veterans Day

VASAVA CALENDAR 2014

Design   VASAVA

Twaddle. Piffle. Nonsense. Whimsy. 365 silly things together in a collection of irrelevant data that you surely knew nothing about nor need to!

Calendaedr

Studio VOKAMA
Design Vladimir Masyuk

This project is based on the thme of dodecahedron. I decided to construct a calendar in the form of dodecahedron using different materials — wood, aluminium and Plexiglass. At the base of dodecahedron structure is a carton frame. Manufactured with laser engraving and laser cutting, and was initially created as a New Year present for 2014.

Matchbook Calendars

Studio Inkello®
Design Christine Schneider
Photography Christine Schneider

For the past five years, I've created a pocket-sized annual calendar which I print using my hand-powered letterpress. I design a different cover each year, and print each month on an individual, perforated page inside. They're each collated and stapled by hand to resemble a matchbook. As each month passes, the page can be torn out to reveal the next month. It's been a signature piece for my letterpress collection each year, and has grown a following around the world. The tradition of creating an annual calendar began during my childhood when I would help my grandfather print self-promotional calendars for his letterpress shop. I'm enjoying carrying on the tradition as a fourth-generation letterpress printer.

NOV 15

Day of the Imprisoned Writer

Calendar 2013

Design Relay Room

For our Relay Room Calendar this year, we conceptualized an unconventional calendar, in the form of an A1 wall poster.

It's peppered with quirky, tongue-in-cheek zodiacal illustrations (we're not true believers in astrology, if you're wondering!). There is more than meets the eye, so you really got to give it a closer look to get in on a chuckle or two (Merlion and X-wings feature in somehow!).

2014 Astrology Calendar

Studio Folk Studio
Design Chelsey Dyer
Photography Chelsey Dyer

"If the stars should appear but one night every thousand years, how man would marvel and adore." — R.W. Emerson

The calendar includes each of the twelve astrological months, as well as their corresponding constellation and moon phases. Printed on 100% post consumer recycled paper, offset printed with soy-based inks.

Ando Calendar — The Twelve of '13

Studio Walvis & Mosmans
Design Tjeerd Walvis, Marc Mosmans, Wijnand de Vries, Aernout Tas, Nina Rödner
Printing Ando Bv

The Ando calendar is an annual gift from the The Hague-based printer, Ando, to it's clients. This year's design and concept, by Walvis & Mosmans, shows the virtues of printing, binding and design like no other. All 2,000 copies were hand bound to create a unique piece of craftsmanship, that is surprising in many different ways. Containing twelve separate sections, the book emphasizes the passing of the year, each month with it's own pattern and colour scheme.

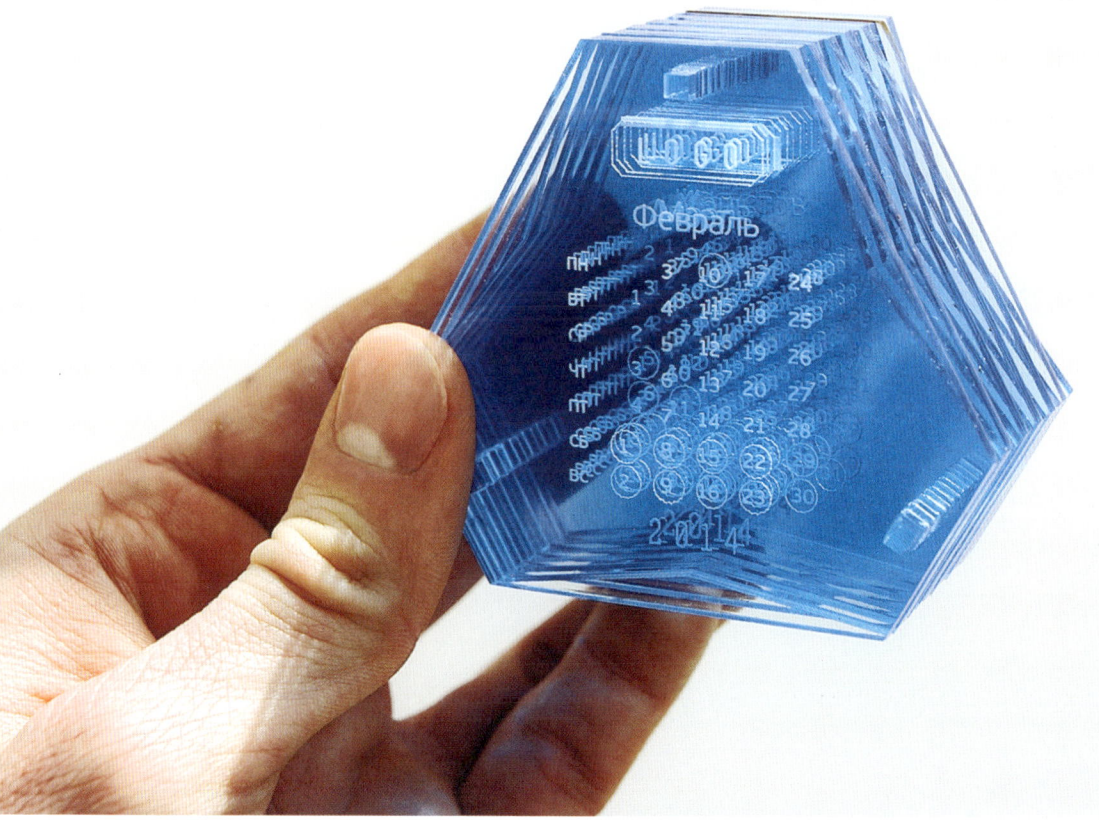

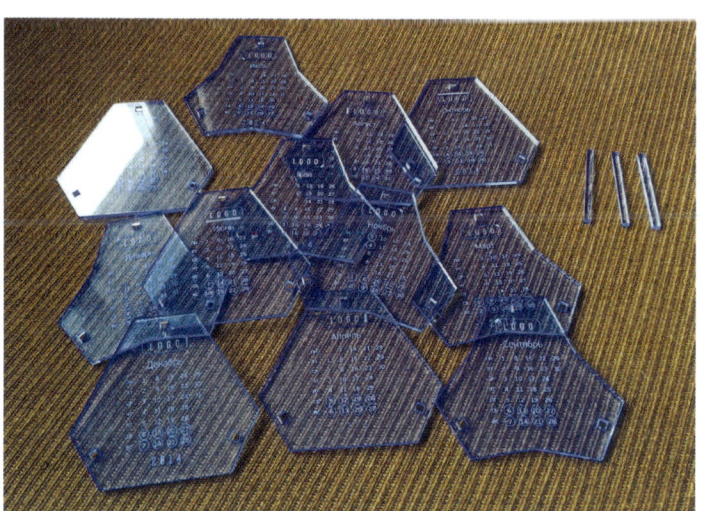

Ice Sandwich Calendar

Studio VOKAMA
Design Vladimir Masyuk

Calendar designed like mini-meccano. The current month is on the first plate, while the others can be seen beneath. As the same modular grid is used, a 3D-effect is attained. To change the month, you need to take off the front plate and fix it at the back of the calendar. The materials used are fluorescent Plexiglas, engraved and cut by laser.

Tonantzin & The Virgin of Guadalupe Calendar 2012

Studio Manuel Olmo
Design Manuel Olmo Rodríguez

This calendar explores the symbolism and stories behind these two very important figures in the cultural development — life and beliefs of the people of Mexico. The year is divided into two halves to be shared by both deities, presenting the coexistence and interlapping of ideologies and cultures.

NOV
21

World Television Day

Letterpress Animal Calendar 2014 — The Bonding

Studio   ditto ditto
Design   p.s. chan

A self-assembled standing calendar, and letterpress printed on 100% cotton paper. Inspired by my friends and families who started their brand new lives as parents. Each month comes with a baby animal — with it's parents showing the love, intimacy and care of family — to remind us the love of parenthood in our nature.

Monthly Measure

Design   Sebastian Bergne
Photography   Sebastian Bergne, L'Atelier d'exercices

The monthly measure calendar is intended as a physical manifestation of days passing. The cast metal cog is manually rolled along the serrated edge of the wooden ruler block.

In today's digital world, I believe that creating physical interactions and routines is important, even if the task could be easily automated. The ruler function is secondary but nevertheless, it is important in adding to the objects depth and identity as a measuring object. Manufactured by Atelier d'Exercises in beach wood and cast aluminium (2011)

NOV 23

International Day to End Impunity

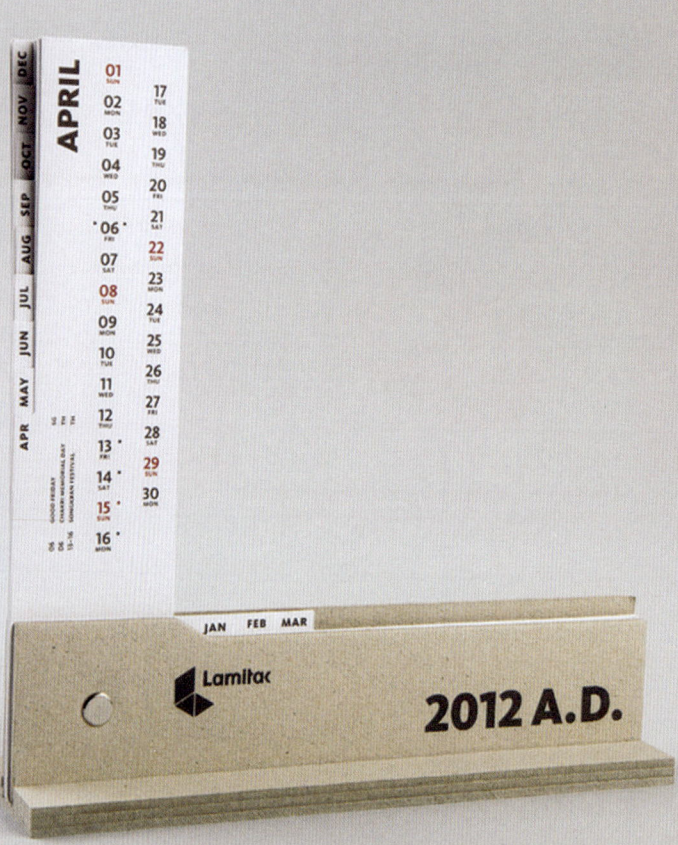

Lamitak Calendar 2012

Studio   Bureau for the Advancement of Lifestyle and Longevity and Success

Inspired by the flip chart for sample swatches, we designed a calendar that stands on its own, yet depicts a modern enough aesthetic to befit the Lamitak brand.

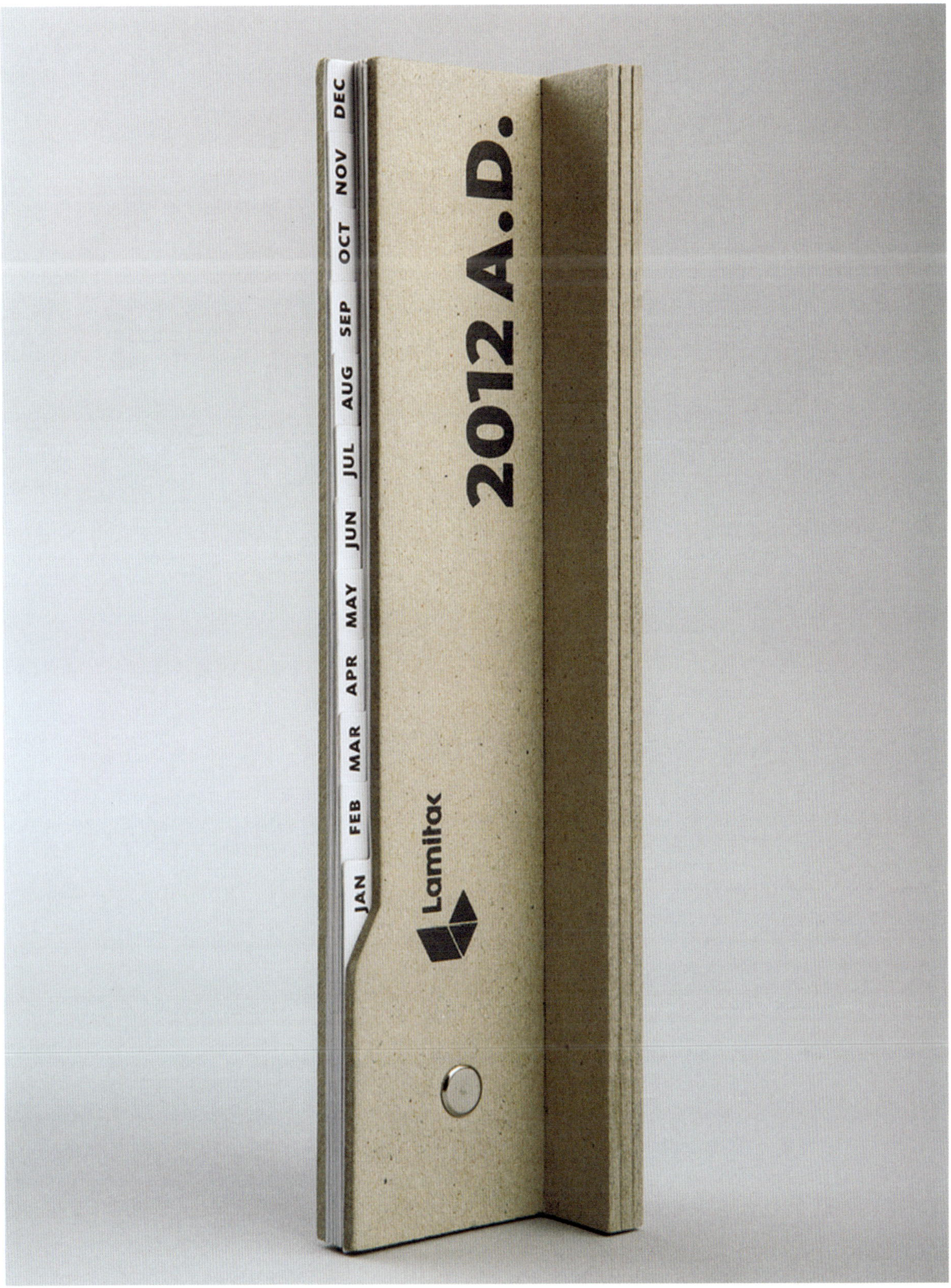

NOV 25

International Day for the Elimination of Violence against Women

Ring Calendar

Design Sebastian Bergne
Photography Sebastian Bergne,
L'Atelier d'exercices

The Ring Calendar is an analogue, interactive wall object that marks the passing of time. Its design is reminiscent of automated clocks or astrological objects from the past. This contrast between the expected "automatic" function and the real manual operation is at the heart of the object. To fully enjoy the Ring Calendar, one must enjoy taking the time to move the ring one notch everyday. Manufactured by Atelier d'Exercises in printed and cut MDF in 2011.

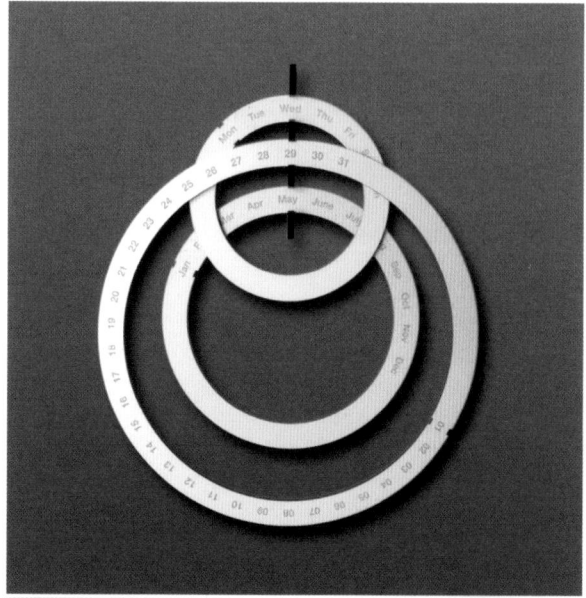

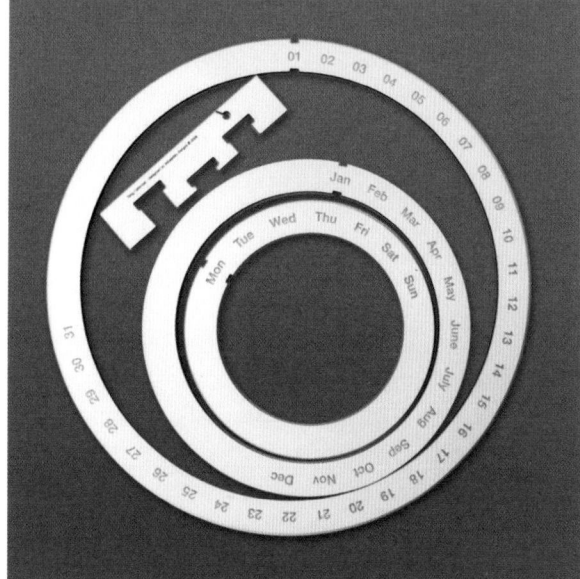

Art Print Japan (A.P.J.)

Studio Homework
Photography Homework

Typographical calendar design for Art Print Japan designed by Homework.

Hand Painted Calendar

Studio Adequate People
Design Elina Zolotareva
Photography Elina Zolotareva

In the age of technology, design studio "Adequate people" created a compliment for its customers — a stylish, graphic calendar drawn by hand. Intricate architectural ornament with fantastic scenes decorate the cardboard backing with dates in the very middle. These are the designer's hand and heart in this unique gift and she did not limit herself in these themes.

MONO 2014

Design Tomasz Kaczkowski

Hot sausages, wild foxes truck drivers, pig's head on the table and all topped with beer and cigarettes absurd sauce.

NOV 29

International Day of Solidarity with the Palestinian People (International)

numerario

Studio   muschi&licheni design network
Art Direction   Marcello Signorile, Eleonora Parise
Design   Francesco Delrosso, Saverio Rociola
Photography   Francesco Delrosso, Saverio Rociola

The "numerario" is a tool designed to order your time in an temporary way. It's a table calendar made of only numbers, without days, months and years and it is always on time. It is divided into units that you can combine together along with different numbers that have been designed intentionally. It comes in four languages: French, English, Italian and German.

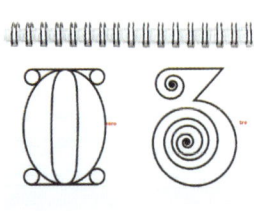

DEC 1

World AIDS Day

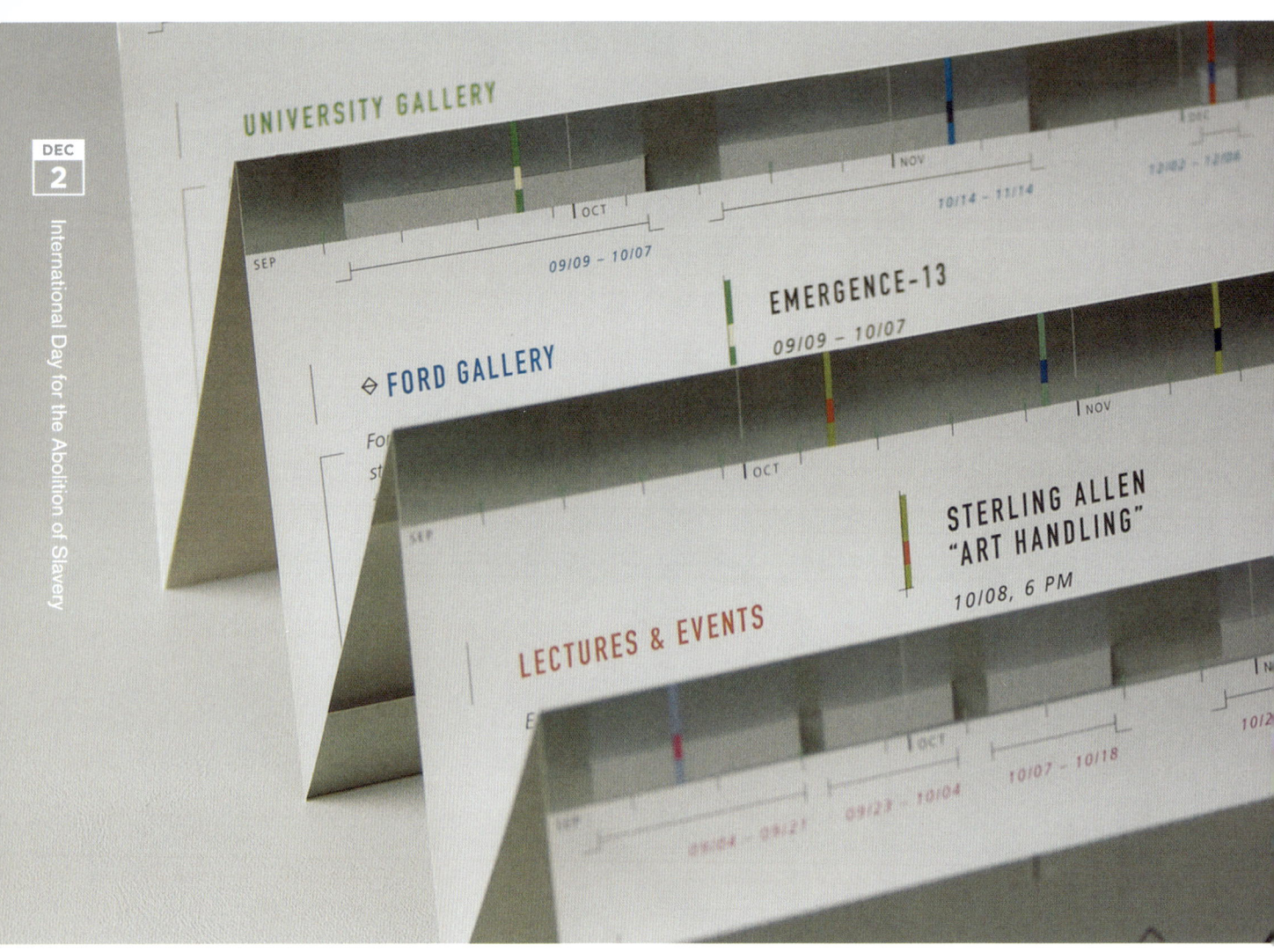

F13GC

Design Bonnie Lobbestael, Lily Sun
Photography Bonnie Lobbestael

The design for the Fall 2013 Gallery Calendar (F13GC) is built on the organization of content. There are four categories of gallery events that are divided using folds. Each category has an individual time-line. The time-lines are aligned when the piece is folded and the duration of each event can be seen in relation to the others. The piece opens to expand the information, showing descriptions and details. The bars on the time-line correspond to the individual events in the interior. Photographs of the work are displayed during each event appear on the opposite side. A 3-D flowchart, constructed from folded paper, frames the images.

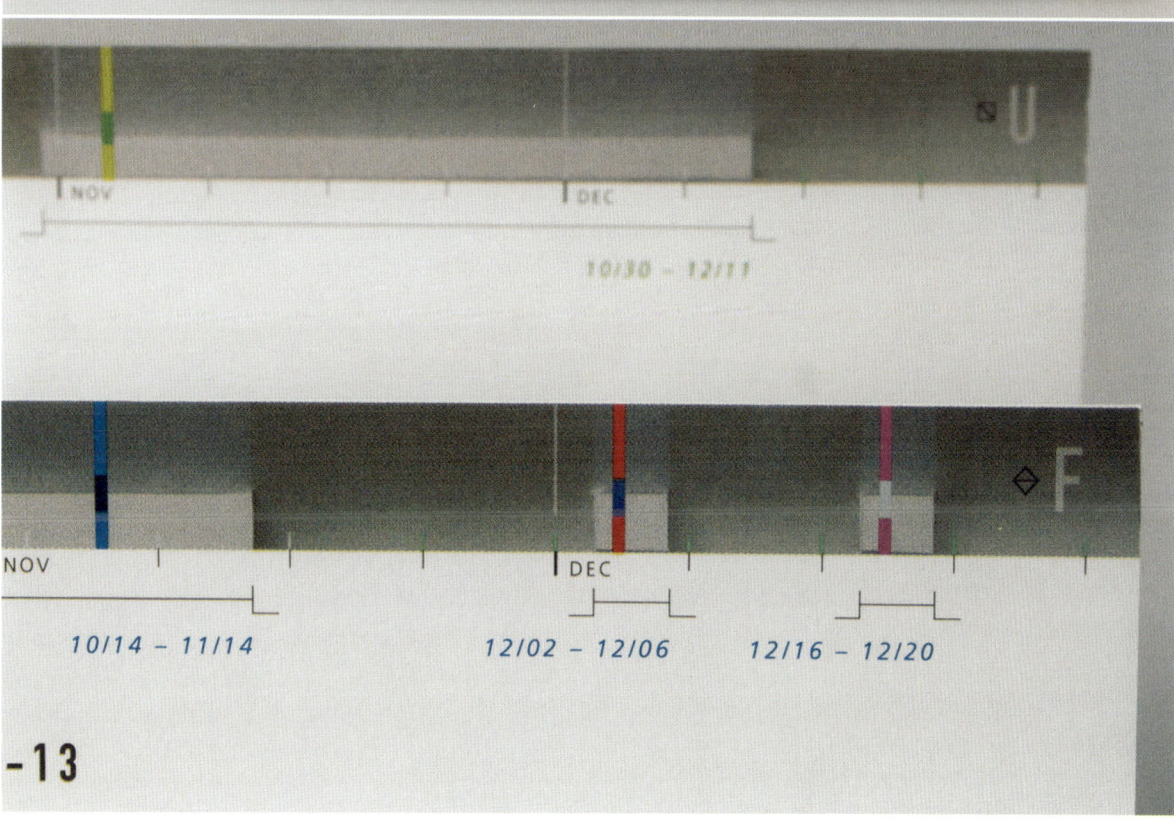

Thai Environment Day (Thailand)

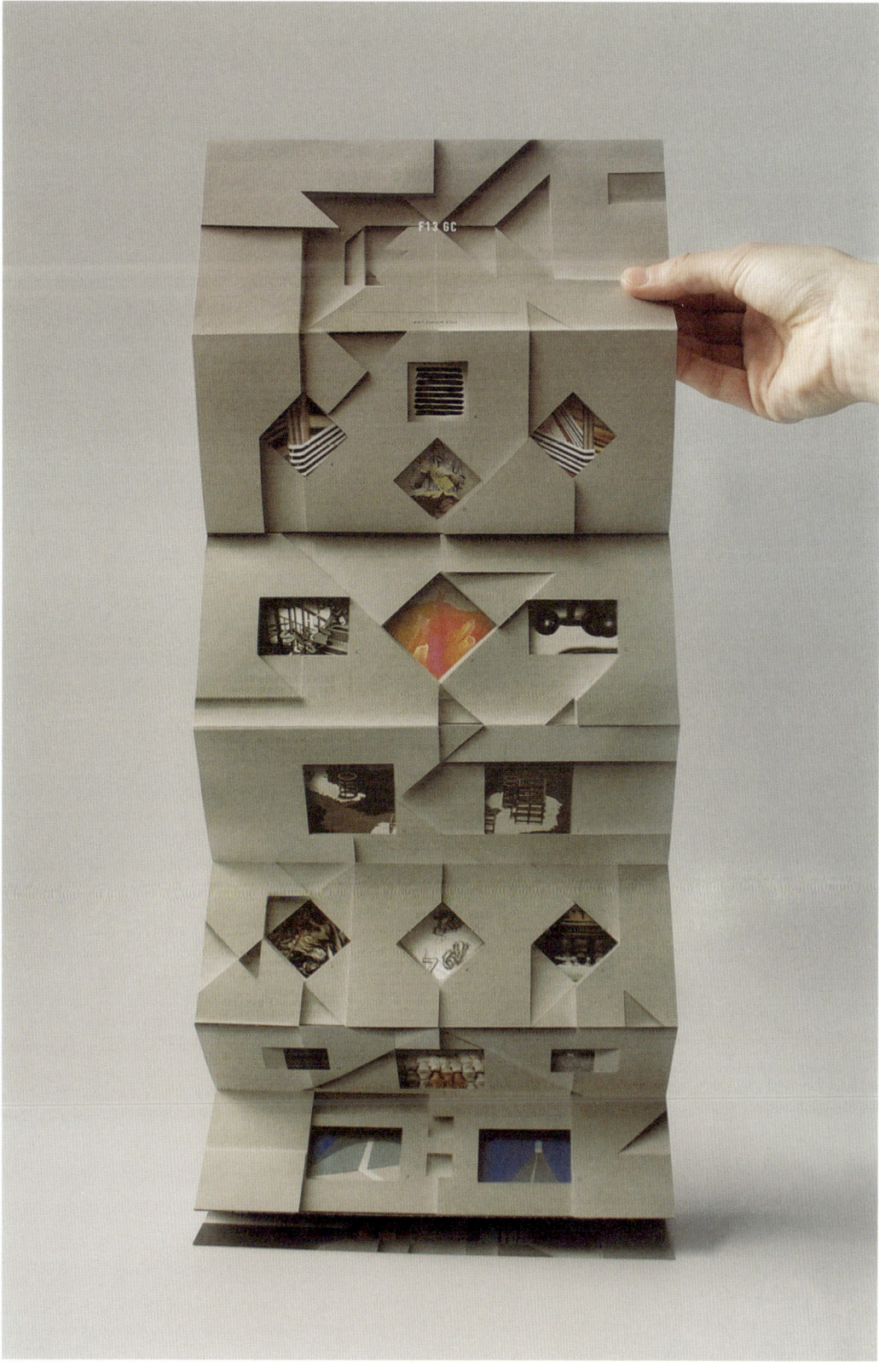

DEC 5

International Volunteer Day

Letterpress Perpetual Calendar

Design Familia Plómez
Photography Juanjo López

Elegant perpetual calendar that will give a touch of distinction and personality to even the most depressing of environments.

Provided with movable parts for individual tens, units, months and days of the week. They skilfully fitted in a traditional and sturdy napkin dispenser, which serves both as a container and as an amazing aesthetic counterpoint.

Module

Studio good morning inc.
Art Direction Katsumi Tamura
Design Takahiro Sugawara
Copy-writing Toshiyuki Nagamatsu

The Module is a useful three-month calendar with individual pieces that may be combined as three cube-shaped stacking modules, so you can assemble them freely at your convenience.

Quality designs have the power to modify space and transform the minds of its users. They offer comfort of seeing, holding and using. They are imbued with lightness and an element of surprise, enriching space. Our original products are designed using the concept of Life with Design.

DEC 7

International Civil Aviation Day

2014 WK Goodness Calendar

Studio — WK Goodness
Design — Justin Flood (Jan), Ben Clark (Feb), Sarah Hollowood (Mar), Rehanah Spence (Apr), Paul Levy (May), Patrick Nistler (Jun), Thomas Bradley (Jul), Allison Berg (Aug), Helena McMurchie (Sep), Mike Weihs (October), Joe Limauro (Nov), Ben Guernsey (Dec), Brad Simon (Cover)
Screen-printing — Kevin Shaw

Each year, our studio releases a limited edition custom calendar to celebrate our talents. Each month is designed by a different studio artist. Using our risograph printer, each designer was asked to create a design unique to their respective month using a uniform two-colour palette. The matchbook cover was screen-printed and each calendar was assembled and trimmed by hand.

Happy New Year 2012–2014

Design Marianne Beck

A self-initiated project, a Happy-New-Year-poster which serves as a calendar as well. It is decorative as well as functional, and the client will think of me throughout the whole year!

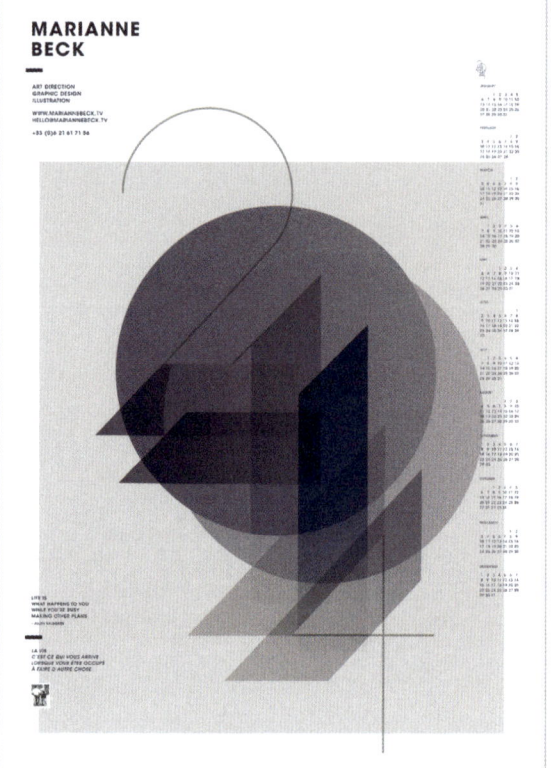

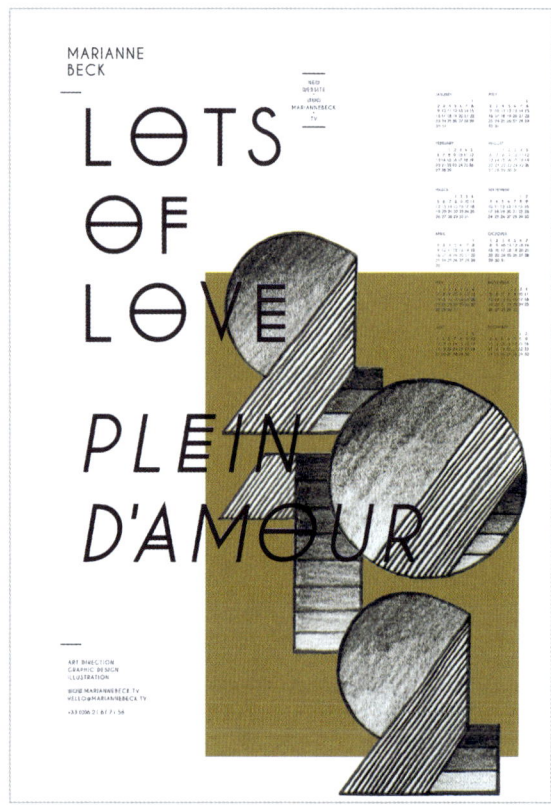

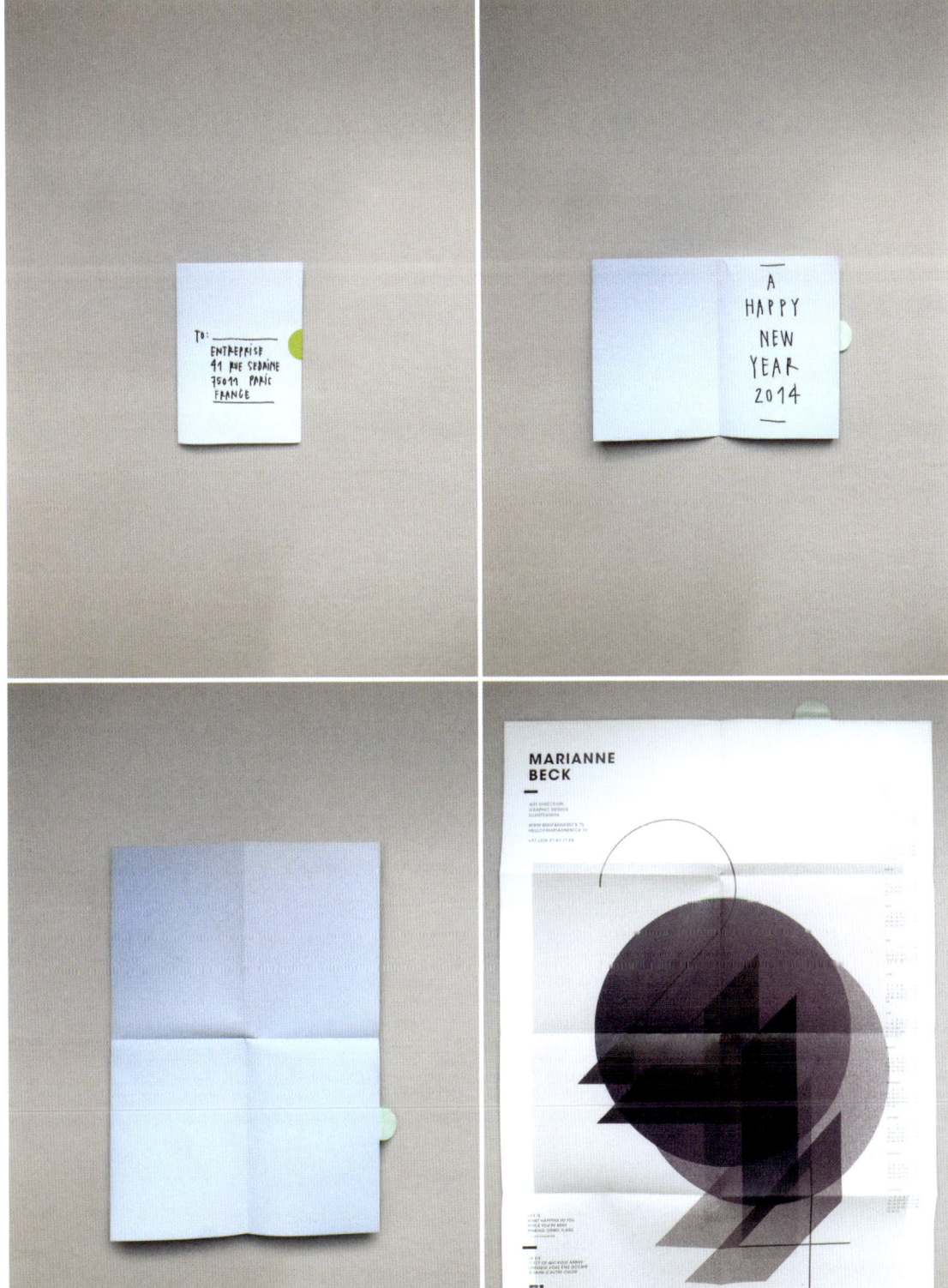

Instituto Asturiano De Prevención De Riesgos Laborales 2014

Studio SANTAMARINA DISEÑADORES
Design José Santamarina

Die cutting and folded desk calendars for INSTITUTO ASTURIANO DE PREVENCIÓN DE RIESGOS LABORALES.

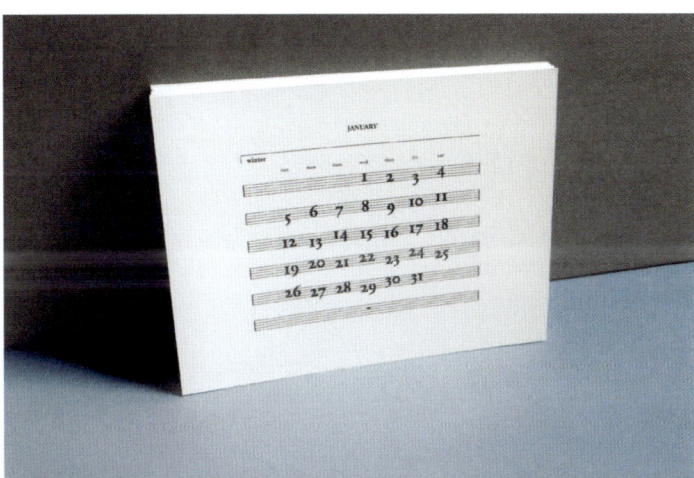

NEWWORK Calendar 2014

Studio   STUDIO NEWWORK
Design   Ryotatsu Tanaka, Ryo Kumazaki, Hitomi Ishigaki

STUDIO NEWWORK has created a 2014 desktop calendar that looks like a music score. This peaceful calendar features 12 monthly cards (including cover page) with an envelope. By marking a date and writing a message on the cards, you can also use them as message cards for birthdays, anniversaries, and other special events.

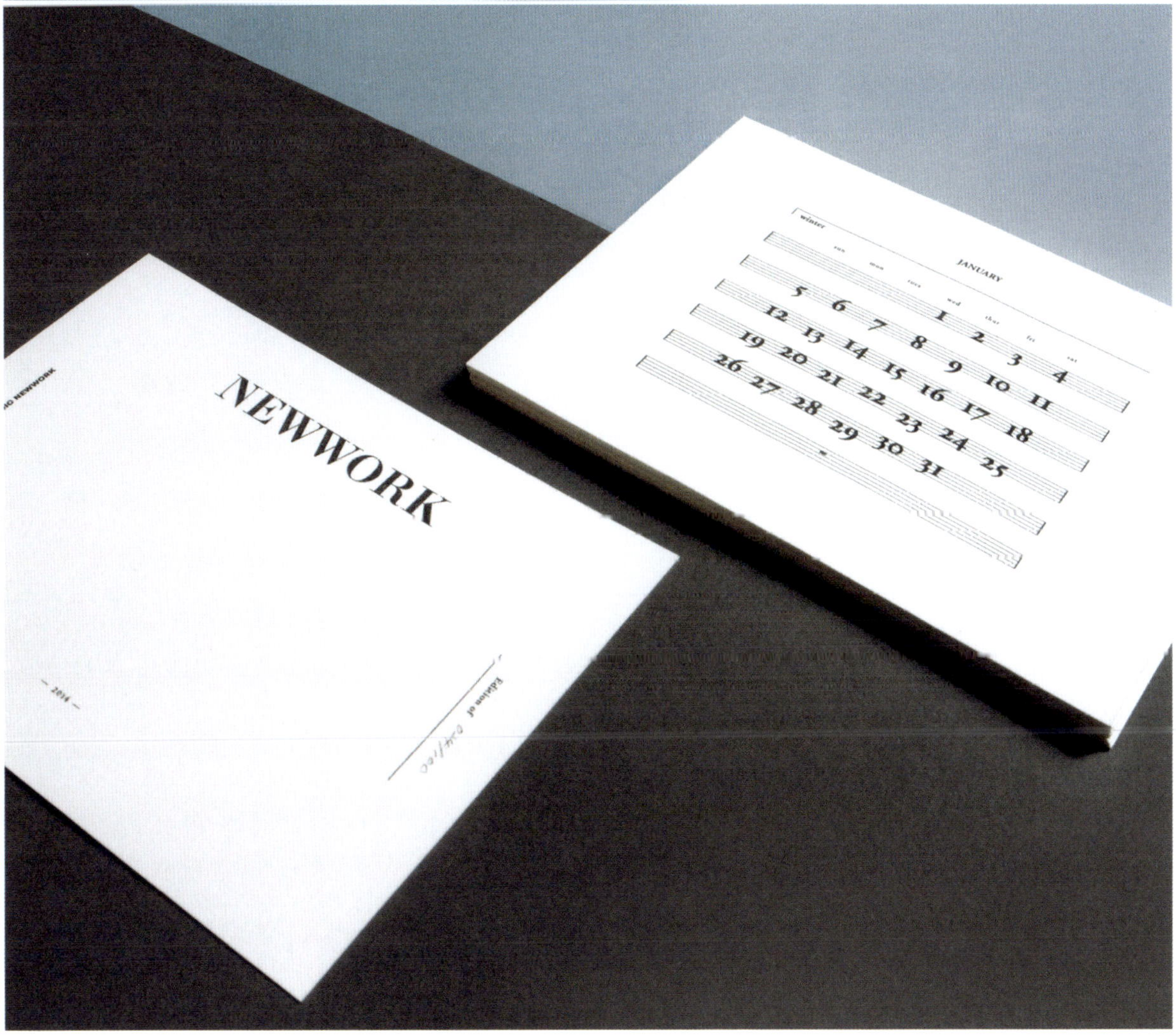

DEC
13

Republic Day (Malta)

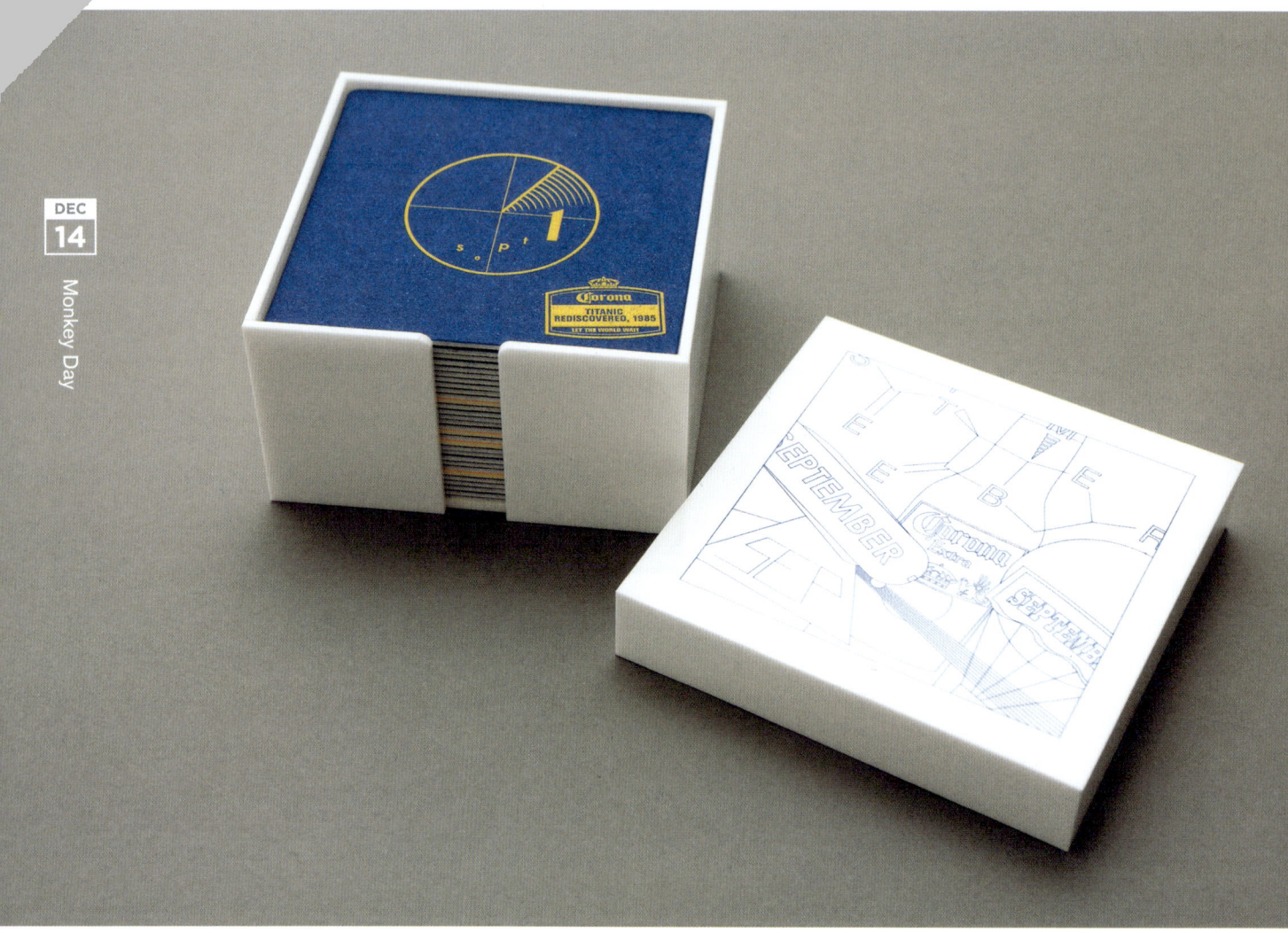

The Corona Calendar

Agency — TBWA\ Singapore
Creative Direction — Gary Steele, Hagan de Villiers
Concept — Nuno Teixeira, Reginald Ocampo, James Holman
Design — Nuno Teixeira, Gary Steele, Reginald Ocampo, Max Kitaev, Aaron Tan, Daphne Tann, Roger Tan, Cheng Guan Koh, Kevin Sim
Account Management — June Wee, Elyn Ong, Lauren Britton
Production — Haydn Evans, Peter Short, Peter Ng, Andrew Yeoh & Raul Davadilla
Photography — Renjie Teo

The world's biggest beer brands are fighting for a share in South East Asia. Caught somewhere in the middle is the distributor. And the distributor is ultimately the key to success — because if he loves your brand, he'll push it in bars, which means that consumers will love your brand too.

Seems simple enough, right? But when you don't have the money to outspend your competitors, or constantly equip distributors with tiresome promotions and costly sales incentives, you need to find another way to keep them thinking about your brand.

The Corona Calendar is a daily reminder to find some time to put your feet up, crack a Corona and let the world wait. But it is also 365 individual ideas for parties or promotions that a distributor can create with Corona. Parties draw crowds. Crowds make money. And distributors do like money. Simple right?

DEC
15

Bill of Rights Day (United States)

National Sports Day (Thailand)

DEC
17

Wright Brothers Day

International Migrants Day

Skirt-Flipping Calendar

Design   Kaori Kato

"Skirt-flipping"; the act of lifting up a girl's skirt to glance at her panties, and a typical pre-adolescent schoolboy's fantasy in Japan. As with most such fantasies, it is rarely acted upon but often referred to in popular culture.

The "Skirt-Flipping Calendar" takes its motif from this forbidden playground game, where the image of a high-school girl's skirt forms the calendar pages of each month. As you turn over or "flip" each page, you will see a different skirt for that particular month. That is, you won't get to see her panties so easily.

Designed by women, this calendar has been a hit with both sexes. Enjoy "skirt-flipping" whether at home or at work, but don't turn all the pages at once; have patience, for good things come to those who wait and persevere. Flip one skirt-page per month and find a pleasant surprise at the end of the year!

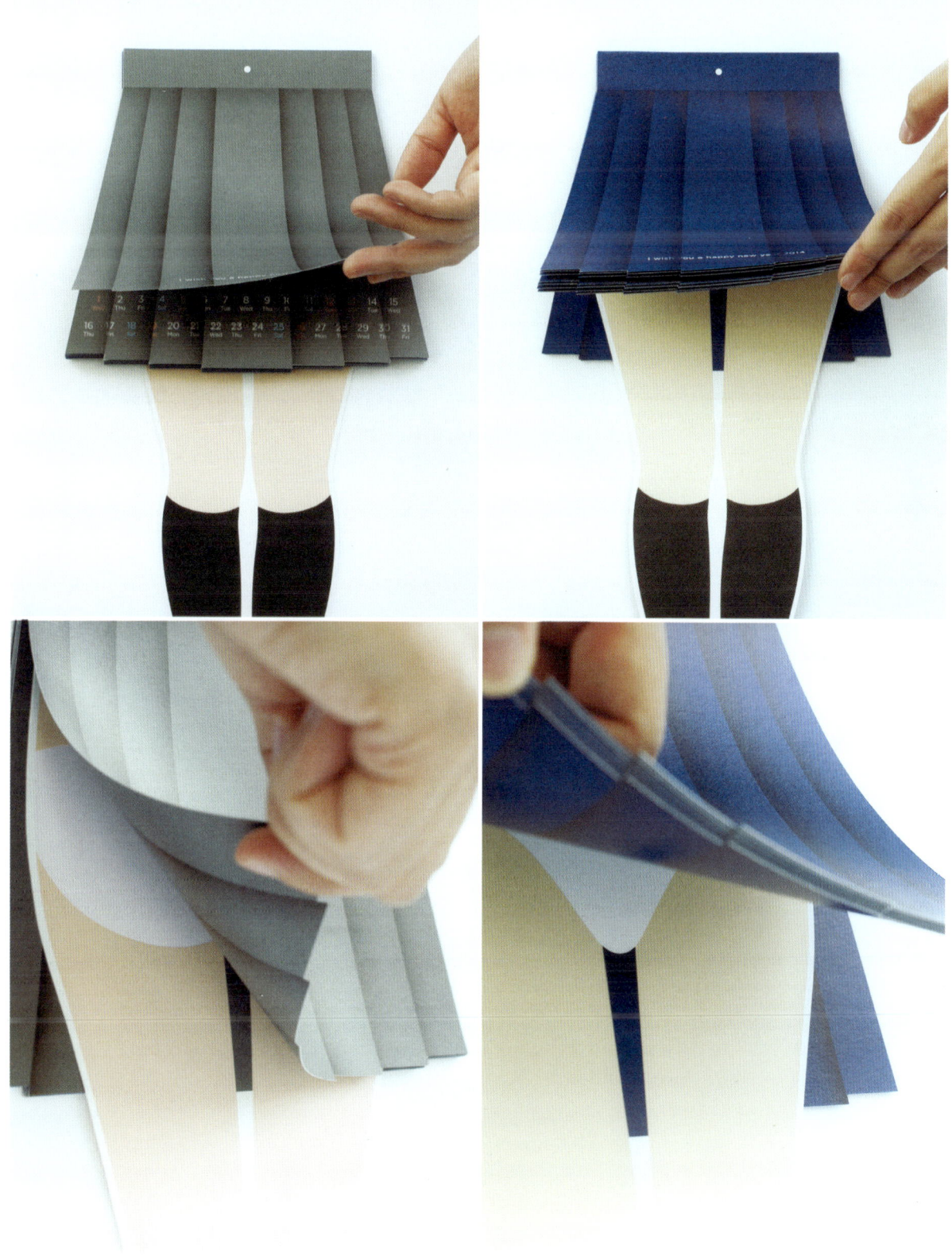

DEC
19

Liberation day (Goa)

Night Calendar

Design Maria Deligiorgi
Printing Tind
Photography Marilia Fotopoulou,
Maria Deligiorgi

This is a pretty unique, unusual wall poster calendar. Instead of helping you count the days, it helps you count the nights of your year, by being a normal (yet mysterious) poster during the day, and by showing you the dates only during the night. It absorbs any kind of light and glows up in the dark. It works perfectly in black light, too. It is silkscreen printed, strictly limited to 70 copies in total. Some versions have a special, custom made sparkling black ink, and some versions with metallic purple ink, while all versions have the amazing phosphorescent ink. Depending on the version, the printing surface was either Munken Polar 240 gsm, or recycled paper 240 gsm; transparent sticker, or white sticker; or transparent PVC or White PVC, 0.3mm.

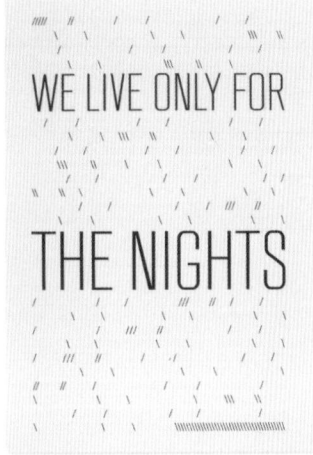
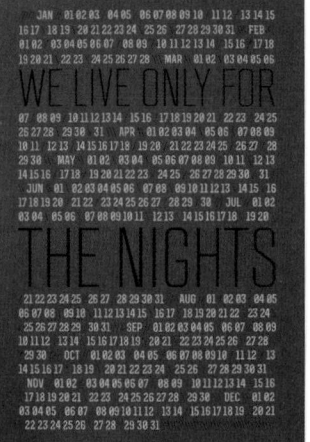
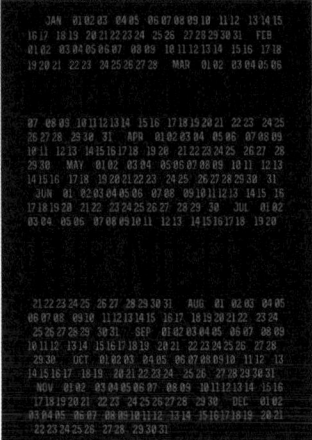

Calendario de los días mundiales

Design Soom Studio

There are many different calendars in the world and many strange things to celebrate. In this calendar, we show these strange unusual days, which actually exist, as all of them are celebrated somewhere in the world on the day shown in the calendar. There were only 200 paper copies of the calendar made but the online version can be accessed and enjoyed by anyone at http://diasmundiales.com.

What is more, pieces of merchandising like mugs and t-shirts, were made to go with the calendar. The project is the brainchild of Guille Viglione, and is a present for Dimension's clients, and we at Soom Studio carried out the artwork. This particular work and some others may be seen at www.soomstudio.com.

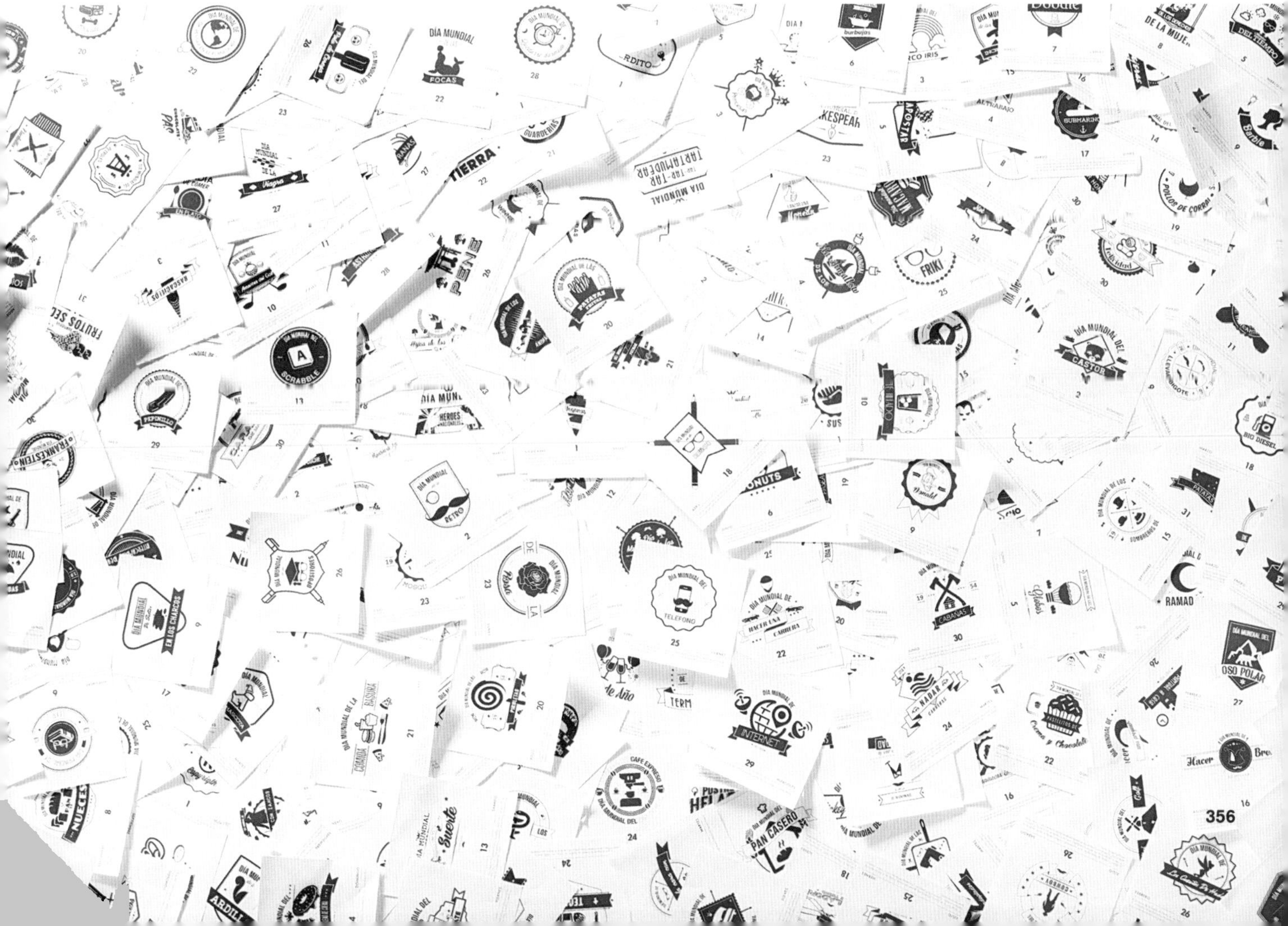

DEC 21

Forefathers' Day (Plymouth, Massachusetts)

DEC
22

National Mathematics Day (India)

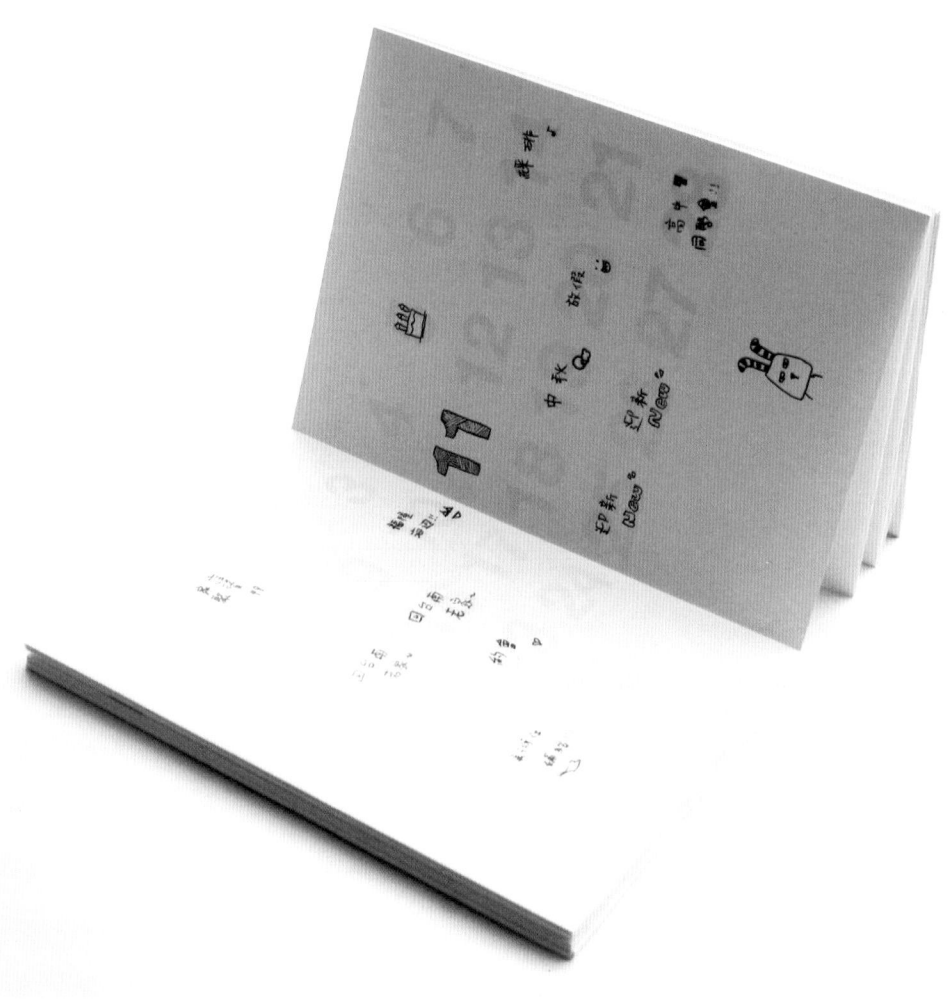

Invisible Calendar

Studio   Sashapure
Design   Sasha Tseng

What are the important information on a calendar that needs to stand out?

For Invisible Calendar, besides events, other days will be invisible. The dates on Invisible Calendar are printed with clear ink and looks like a plain paper. However, if you write down your important events, they can be seen crystal clear since all of the unimportant information is "invisible". Also, Invisible Calendar could be easily opened to show all 12 months at once — it's a new perspective to see the entire year on one page. It's fun to look back on the year and see all the events that occurred. On the reverse side, the calendar is blank and can be used as a notepad, giving people more space to write down their daily activities or notes. This simplistic and minimal design allows for more creative freedom to write and draw as people wish. This pocketbook size allows you to carry it anywhere and show off your individual interpretations of your activities.

DEC 23

Children's Day (South Sudan)

DEC 24

Christmas Eve

IN-DEX

DEC 25 — Christmas Day

Boxing Day

#

&LARRY
www.andlarry.com

XTRA Calendar 2013 — 295

3EYEDBEAR
3eyedbear.com

Camouflage — 19
Time is Precious — 145

3NITY
www.3nitydesign.com

Orna Paper Calendar — 135

A

ADEQUATE PEOPLE
www.adekvate.com

Hand Painted Calendar — 333
Many Happy Dragons of The Year — 157
Patties* About Artiodactyl's Life — 8

AINORWEI LIN
www.behance.net/Ainorwei_Lin

Natural (2014 Calendar) — 105

ALAN DANBY
www.behance.net/alan-danby

Fedrigoni Calendar 2015 — 289

ALEXANDER SCHIERL
www.schierl.de

Systemform Kalender 2014 — 277

ALEXIS BOURCERET
www.behance.net/alexisbourceret

Typographic Calendar — 243

AMELIA KRYSZTOFIAK
www.behance.com/amelia.krysztofiak

Square the Circle — 279

ANJE JAGER
anjejager.com

Systemform Kalender 2014 — 277

AVRIL LORETI / MODERN HOME
avrilloreti.com

Calendar Tea Towels — 49

AZUL PIÑEIRO
be.net/azulpineiro

2013 Friends Calendar — 301

B

BEL'S ART WORLD
www.belsartworld.com

Illustrative Calendar 2014 — 109

BESSERMACHEN DESIGNSTUDIO
www.bessermachen.com

Chocolates With Attitude 2011 — 269

BITRI
bybitri.com

Past & Future Calendar — 233

BONNIE LOBBESTAEL
bonnielobbestael.com

F13GC — 337

BRANDBERRY
www.brandberry.net

Stampd — 41

BUNCH
www.bunchdesign.com

Allegheny Financial 2012 — 35
Allegheny Financial 2013 — 185

BUREAU FOR THE ADVANCEMENT OF LIFESTYLE AND LONGEVITY AND SUCCESS
www.thebureau.com.sg

Lamitak Calendar 2012 — 329

BUSYBUILDING
www.busybuilding.com

12 Little Monsters — 121
Design Invaders — 131
No Matter How Many Skies Have Fallen — 179

C

CALVIN TAN
www.behance.net/calvintandou

Gong Xi Fa Cai — 255

CARLOS HIGUERA
carloshiguera.net

2013 Friends Calendar — 301
Homeless Monsters Calendar 2012 — 127

CAROL MCLEOD DESIGN
www.carolmcleoddesign.com

TODAY IS A HOLIDAY! COASTER SET — 193

CÁTIA SÁ
www.behance.net/catiasaillustration

Calendar Kids 2014 — 51

CCRZ
www.ccrz.ch

Gruppo Giovani Industriali Como Calendar — 199

CHELSEA PHILLIPS
*behance.net/chelseaphillips_*

Calendar Card Deck — 21

CHIII DESIGN LTD.
www.chiiidesign.com

IC Calendar Design — 133

361

CHRIS ONG
chrisongdesign.squarespace.com

Fedrigoni Calendar 2015　　　211

COMME UNE IMAGE
www.carlacascales.com
www.commeuneimage.es

Comme une image Calendar　　　187

CONRAD THERON

The World's Most Eco-Friendly Calendar　　　267

CORN STUDIO
www.cornstudio.gr

The Astrozodiac Calendar　　　189

CRISPIN FINN
www.crispinfinn.com

Year Planner 2014　　　25

CURIOUSDOODLES
www.curiousdoodles.com

2013 Tea Towel Calendar　　　244
2013 Wall Calendar: Succulent
　　Paper Cut Poster　　　162
2014 Wood Veneer Calendar　　　266

CYCLOS DESIGN GMBH
www.cyclos-design.de

WORLD'S FESTIVALS — ON PAPER　　　113

D

DAN USISKIN
www.danusiskin.com

Dot to Date　　　229

DANIEL TING CHONG
www.danieltingchong.com

Almanac Calender　　　207

DANKA GRALIK
dankagralik.com

Seed Calendar　　　137

DIG / PLUS GMBH
www.populaere-produkte.de

Wandplaner & Wandkalender　　　15

DIGITPROP
www.digitprop.com

Stegosaurus Paper-craft Calendar　　　100

DIMA SERGEEV
dimasergeev.com

IZOLYATSIA 2013　　　215

DITTO DITTO
www.dittoditto.net

Letterpress Animal Calendar 2014 —
　　The Bonding　　　327

DMG
www.dmgdmg.ru

Sugar for Everyday　　　212

E

EGGHEAD
www.thinkegghead.com

Calendar EGGHEAD 2013　　　163

ELIASDESIGN.RU
www.eliasdesign.ru

The Concept of Corporate
　　Calendar of Plastic　　　38

EMILIJA UŽUKAUSKIENE
www.behance.net/emilija_u

2014 Desktop Calendar for ANTALIS　　　93

ERIC CHAN, JACKY WONG
www.ericchandesign.com

Polytrade Calendar Memo　　　209

ERMAKOV SERGEY
code501.net

City Calendar　　　115

F

FABIAN GREISER
www.fabiangreiser.com

Run Run Run Calendar　　　123

FABIEN BARRAL
www.mr-cup.com

The Creative Manifesto　　　183

FAMILIA PLÓMEZ
www.familiaplomez.com

Letterpress Perpetual Calendar　　　341

FILIP NEMET
thisisbullsheep.com

Eco Gif Package　　　77

FOLK STUDIO
www.folkstudio.co

2014 Astrology Calendar　　　322

FOOOLISH DESIGNERS
www.fooolish.com

Interactive Calendar 2013　　　87

FUUFF
www.behance.net/fuuff

Hua　　　205

G

GIULIA DE ROSSI
www.derossigiula.com

Woodstock is Not:
　　2015 Desk Calendar for Fedrigoni　　　151

DEC 27

Emergency Rescuer's Day (Russia)

362

GONÇALO CAMPOS
www.goncalocampos.com

| Dia Calendar | 311 |

GOOD MORNING INC.
www.goodmorning.co.jp

Botanical Life	53
Farm	62
Flowers	57
Module	342
Safari	26
Town	27

H

HAMPER STUDIO, LABORATORIUM
www.hamper.hr

| Periodic Table of Time | 298 |

HARALD GEISLER
haraldgeisler.com

| 2014 Typographic Wall Calendar | 46 |

HEATHER LINS
www.heatherlinshome.com

| Stitch the Stars Calendar Kit | 236 |
| Year in Stitches Calendar Kit | 235 |

HILGER & BOIE DESIGN
www.hilger-boie.de

| 1:X – Twelve Looks Through the Magnifying Glass | 65 |

HOMEWORK
www.homework.dk

| Art Print Japan (A.P.J.) | 332 |
| Paustian | 166 |

I

INKELLO®
www.inkello.com

| Matchbook Calendars | 319 |

IRFAN GHANI

| The World's Most Eco-Friendly Calendar | 267 |

ISADORA GONZAGA
www.behance.net/isadoragonzaga

| Calendar ADG | 253 |

J

JENNITA SHAH
www.behance.net/jennitashah

| Pull Up Yourself to Face New Challenges | 89 |

JESSE BRAY

| The World's Most Eco-Friendly Calendar | 267 |

JIHYE LEE
www.behance.net/thisisjihyelee

| Fedrigoni 2015 Calendar | 156 |

JODIE-ANN LANGLEY
cargocollective.com/jodieannlangley

| Fedrigoni Desk Calendar 2015 | 95 |

JOLLYGOODFELLOW
www.jollygoodfellow.se

| urbnCal 2013 NORDIC | 291 |

JUDY KAUFMANN
www.judykaufmann.com

| Calendar 2014 | 161 |

K

KAORI KATO
design.kaorikato.com

| Skirt-Flipping Calendar | 353 |

KEVIN REINALDO ARFFANDY
www.behance.net/kevinranting

| 2000+12 Calendar | 177 |

KK OUTLET
www.kkoutlet.com

| The Standard Hotel Calendar | 257 |

KOAY YEE SHIN
www.behance.net/dennis_koay

| Gong Xi Fa Cai | 255 |

KOLLE REBBE GMBH
www.kolle-rebbe.de

| The Scent Of Time | 305 |
| The Tea Calendar | 313 |

KOSTANTIA MANTHOU
kostantiamanthou.com

| Fragile Pocket Calendar | 217 |

L

LAURA WALLBRIDGE-BRUCE
www.behance.net/laurawallbridgebruce

| YCN Fedrigoni 2015 Desk Calendar | 275 |

LENA ZUERN
cargocollective.com/lenazuern

| Woodstock is Not: 2015 Desk Calendar for Fedrigoni | 151 |

LEO BURNETT
www.leoburnett.co.uk

| Pantone Queen | 293 |

LILIIA PRIADKO
www.behance.net/pryadko

| 25th Frame | 61 |

LO SIENTO
losiento.net

| 2012 Calendar | 107 |

LUCA FONTANA
www.behance.net/lucafontana

| Wall Street English Calendar 2014 | 99 |

M

MAGDALENA THUR
www.magdalenathur.com

DAYZ Weekly Planner — 287

MAKE COLLABORATION
makecollab.com

Vertical Calendar — 153

MANOLAB
www.manolab.it

One Year, One Texture — 299

MANUEL OLMO
manuelolmo.com

Tonantzin & The Virgin of Guadalupe Calendar 2012 — 325

MARGARITA KURTSER
www.behance.net/Ritaku

Calendar of Astronomical Events 2014 — 307
Calendar Transformer Kit 2014 — 173

MARIA DELIGIORGI
www.behance.net/m_del

Night Calendar — 355

MARIANNE BECK
www.mariannebeck.tv

Happy New Year 2012–2014 — 345

MARINA PAVLOVA
www.behance.net/m_dobraya

RuArts Gallery Desk Calendar — 285

MARY MCDERMOTT
marymcdermottdesign.com

Ciao Calendar — 141

MAURESA HANKINSON
www.behance.net/mauresa

My Zoo 2014 — 76

MAUSAM AGGARWAL
www.behance.net/mausamaggarwal

Calendar Designs for the Year of 2014 — 55

MEERA LEE PATEL
www.meeralee.com

2014 Elephant Calendar Tea Towel — 165

MICHAEL AUGSTEN
www.lessthingz.com

DAYZ Weekly Planner — 287

MILK DESIGN LTD.
www.milkdesign.com.hk

Memo Calendar — 171

MINK LETTERPRESS
www.minkletterpress.com

2012 Vintage Handkerchief Calendar — 247
2013 A Dozen Eggs Calendar — 259
2014 Growth & Decay Calendar — 59

MOHIT LAKHMANI
www.behance.net/mohitlakhmani

3D Infographic Calender — 246

MUSCHI&LICHENI DESIGN NETWORK
www.muschielicheni.net

numerario — 335

N

NIKITA IVANOV
www.behance.net/nicknow

Calendar 2014 — 5th Element — 248

NOBLANCO
www.noblanco.com

Gráficas Unidas Calendar — 219
Poster — Calendars 2014 — 91

NOSIGNER
nosigner.com

GREEN CALENDAR — 140

O

OKSANA KAPRANOVA
www.behance.net/KshihaKapranova

Game Calendar 2014 — 283

OLIVER MILLS
www.behance.net/olliemills

Fedrigoni Woodstock Calendar 2015 — 11

ONION DESIGN ASSOCIATES
oniondesign.com.tw

3D Rock Show Calendar — 241
Mos Burger 2010 Calendar — 23

P

PAPER PUSHER
www.jpking.ca
www.paperpusher.ca

2014 Isometric Risograph Calendar — 231

PAULAMASTRA
www.paulamastra.com

Craft&Tech 2013 Calendar — 169

PETER VON FREYHOLD
www.vonfreyhold.com

C|M|Y|K Farbfächer Kalender 2014 — 117

PHAGE LIMITED
www.phagedesign.co.uk

Ideas for the Year — 79

DEC 29

Independence Day (Mongolia)

PHENOMENA
www.phenomena.jo

Phenomenal Calendar — 315

PIXELBOX ESTUDIO GRÁFICO S.L.U.
www.pixelbox.es

2014 CALENDAR — 297
ENJOY YOUR TRIP — 73

POLKKA JAM
www.polkkajam.com

Doggies Wall Calendar for 2014 — 45
Kissanpäivät Wall Calendar for 2013 — 63

POP & ZEBRA
www.popandzebra.com

A Box of Elephants — 195

PROJECT 53
www.p53.co.uk

2015 Calendars — 7

Q

QUBE STUDIO (SINGAPORE)
qubestudio.com

2012 Calendar — 237
Event Matching System Diary — 181

R

RAVEN KIM
www.ravenidea.com

1000 Year Calendar — 67

REBOOT CREATIVE AGENCY
www.reboot.com.gr

Calendar 2013 — 34
Calendar 2014 — 103

REDCRUISER
redcruiser.com

2014 Beer + Food Pairings Calendar — 232

RELAY ROOM
www.relayroom.com

2012 Summer Planner — 9
Calendar 2013 — 321

RETNO HADININGDIAH
behance.net/rhadiningdiah

Bingo Card Calendar — 75

RIDHWAAN MOOLLA
ridhwaanmoolla.com

The Brain — 2013 Novelty Calendar — 309

RYAN HO
www.visitryan.com

Type Calendar — 68

S

SANTAMARINA DISEÑADORES
www.santamarinadg.com

Instituto Asturiano De Prevención
    De Riesgos Laborales 2014 — 347

SASCHA KUNTZE

The World's Most Eco-Friendly Calendar — 267

SASHAPURE
www.sashapure.com

Invisible Calendar — 357

SEBASTIAN BERGNE
www.sebastianbergne.com

Monthly Measure — 328
Ring Calendar — 331

SEOUNGKYEONG LEE
www.behance.net/seungseung

Cup Holder and Calendar — 155

SHKRABA YEKATERINA
behance.net/tekkhi

City Calendar — 115

SIGNORINA NAVARRA | DOO DAA STUDIO
signorinanavarra.com
doodaastudio.com

Tastee Toaster Calendar — 223

SKY GOODIES PRODUCTS AND APPLICATIONS PRIVATE LIMITED
skygoodies.co

Sky Goodies Colourful Miniature
    Typewriter Calendar — 147
Sky Goodies Doodle Monthly Planner — 213
Sky Goodies DIY 3D Landscape Calendar — 138

SNAEFRID & HILDIGUNNUR
snaefrid.is
hildigunnur.is

Perforated Calendar 2014 — 265

SNORRI ELDJÁRN SNORRASON
www.snorrieldjarn.com

Mánatal / Moon Calendar — 64

SNUG.STUDIO
www.snug-online.com

SNUG.TOYBLOCKS 2015 — 33
SNUG.VERTICAL 2015 — 60

SOOM STUDIO
www.soomstudio.com

Calendario de los días mundiales — 356
Calendario Madera — 224

SPECIAL PROJECTS / VITAMINS
www.lego-calendar.com
www.special-projects-studio.com

Bit Planner — 143

STROOMBERG (PHILIP STROOMBERG)
www.stroomberg.net

The Cube Calendar — 97

STUDIO NEWWORK
www.studionewwork.com

NEWWORK Calendar 2014 — 348

STUDIO ON FIRE
studioonfire.com

2014 Studio On Fire Desk Calendar — 159

STUDIO SERVAAS
www.studioservaas.com

Calendar 2015 — 28

T

TAN SAY FIN
www.behance.net/fintan_belle

Gong Xi Fa Cai — 255

TATSUYA TANAKA
miniature-calendar.com

MINIATURE CALENDAR — 29

TBWA\ SINGAPORE
tbwa.com.sg

The Corona Calendar — 349

THAIS NAVARRO
estudiosortido.com

Calendarinhos — 167

THE CONSERVANCY ASSOCIATION
www.cahk.org.hk

CAreLender 2014 — 201

THE FINGERSMITH
www.thefingersmithletterpress.com

Dance Like No One is Watching — 101

THE LEO BURNETT DEPT. OF DESIGN
www.leoburnett.com

2014 DoD Calendar — 17

THE LETTERPRESS SHOPPE
letterpressshoppe.com

COLOURFUL: A Letterpress Desk Calendar — 249

THE VISUAL AGENCY
www.thevisualagency.it

A Visual Year — 2014 Calendar — 47

THIS STUDIO
www.this-studio.co.uk

This Year 2014 — 37

TIM WAN
www.timwan.co.uk

Predictions Calendar Series — 69

TOFU STUDIO / POLAND
www.tofu.pl

ETNO (Ethno) — 83
FAIRYTALES 2015 — 239
TANGRAM — 225
WYCINANKA (Paper-Cut) — 261

TOMASZ KACZKOWSKI
kaczkowski.net

MONO 2014 — 334

TÚ BÙI
buiphamthanhtu.com

1735km — 139

U

UPSTRUCT
upstruct.com

upstruct calendar 2013 — 245
upstruct calendar 2014 — 203

V

VASAVA
vasava.com

VASAVA CALENDAR 2014 — 317

VICTOR BRANDING DESIGN CORP
www.victad.com.tw

Happy 12 Month 2010 — 221

VOKAMA
www.vokama.ru

Calendaedr — 318
Ice Sandwich Calendar — 324

W

WALVIS & MOSMANS
www.walvismosmans.nl

Ando Calendar — The Twelve of '13 — 323

WAP-OH!
www.wap-oh.com

Life Calendars: How Was Your Day? — 39
Life Calendars: Love Life, Day by Day — 251

WHISKEY DESIGN
whiskeydesign.com

Beer Salt 2014 Calendar — 31

WK GOODNESS
wkgoodness.com

2013 WK Goodness Calendar — 13
2014 WK Goodness Calendar — 343

WONDER STUFF STUDIO
www.wonderstuffstudio.com

Elanders Calendar 2014 — 50

Z

ZEYNEP ORBAY
www.zeyneporbay.com

Land Rover Topographic Calendar — 149

DEC 31

New Year's Eve

THREE HUNDRED AND SIXTY FIVE
Calendar Designs with a Twist

Idea and Concept by

Curated, Edited and Designed by
Working Title & Co.

Published in 2015 by	First published and distributed by
Sendpoints Publishing Co., Limited	Basheer Graphic Books
Room 15A Block 9, Tsui Chuk Garden	Blk 13, Toa Payoh Lorong 8
Wong Tai Sin, Kowloon, Hong Kong	#06-08, Braddell Tech
Tel: +852-69502452	Singapore 319261
Fax: +852-35832448	Tel: +65 6336 0810
info@sendpoints.cn	Fax: +65 6259 1608
www.sendpoints.cn	abdul@basheergraphic.com
Online shop: shanbents.tmall.com	www.basheergraphic.com

Idea and Concept © 2015 Basheer Graphic Books
Design and Editorial © 2015 Working Title & Co.
The copyright for individual text and design work is held
by the respective designers and contributors.

ISBN 978-988-13835-1-8

All rights reserved. No part of this publication may be reproduced, stored
in any retrieval systems or transmitted, in any form or by any means,
electronic, mechanical, photocopying, recording or otherwise, without prior
permission in writing from the publisher or the copyright owner(s).

The captions and artwork in this book are based on materials supplied by the designers
whose work is included. While every effort has been made to ensure their accuracy,
Basheer Graphic Books does not under any circumstances accept any responsibility
for any errors or omissions. However, the publisher would be pleased, if informed,
to correct any errors or omissions in subsequent editions of this publication.

Printed and bound by
Tiger Printing (Hong Kong) Co. Ltd

Acknowledgements
We would like to thank all the designers and companies involved in the compilation of this
book. This project would not have been accomplished without their significant contribution.
We would also like to express our gratitude to all the producers for their invaluable
opinions and assistance all this time. This book's successful completion also owes a great
deal to many professionals in the creative industry who have provided precious insights
and comments. Lastly to many others whose names, though not credited, who have made
a big impact on our work, we thank you for your continuous support the whole time.

Future Publications
If you would like to contribute to our future publications, please email us at
hello@workingtitleandco.com